Under the Sea Lessons for Life

Teacher + Counselor Activity Guide

Integrating social-emotional growth and academic development

Boys Town, Nebraska

Illustrated by **BRIAN MARTIN**   Written by **SARA KINSEY**

Under the Sea Lessons for Life: Teacher + Counselor Activity Guide Volume 1
Text and Illustrations Copyright © 2024 by Father Flanagan's Boys' Home
ISBN 979-8-88907-019-1

Published by Boys Town Press, 13603 Flanagan Blvd., Boys Town, Nebraska 68010

For a Boys Town Press catalog, call 1-800-282-6657
or visit our website: BoysTownPress.org

Publisher's Cataloging-in-Publication Data

Names: Kinsey, Sara (Sara Elizabeth), author. | Martin, Brian (Brian Michael), 1978- illustrator.

Title: Under the sea lessons for life. Volume 1 : teacher + counselor activity guide: integrating social-emotional growth and academic development / written by Sara Kinsey ; illustrated by Brian Martin.

Identifiers: ISBN: 979-8-88907-019-1

Subjects: LCSH: Success in children--Study and teaching. | Social learning--Study and teaching. | Emotional intelligence--Study and teaching. | Emotions in children--Study and teaching. | Self-control in children--Study and teaching. | Academic achievement--Study and teaching. | Personality and academic achievement--Study and teaching. | Motivation in education-- Study and teaching. | Life skills--Study and teaching. | Social skills--Study and teaching. | Children--Life skills guides--Study and teaching. | BISAC: EDUCATION / Counseling / Academic Development. | EDUCATION / Decision-Making & Problem Solving. | EDUCATION / Counseling/Crisis Management. | EDUCATION / Educational Psychology.

Classification: LCC: BF723.S77 K56 2024 | DDC: 155.4/19--dc23

Printed in the United States
10 9 8 7 6 5 4 3 2 1

Boys Town Press is the publishing division of Boys Town, a national organization serving children and families.

Instructions to download worksheets, handouts, and student storybook

ACCESS:
https://www.boystownpress.org/book-downloads

ENTER:
Your first and last names
Email address
Code: **888907uts0191**
Check yes to receive emails to ensure your email link is received.

SEL STORIES FROM UNDER THE SEA

SOME ACADEMIC LESSONS MAY REQUIRE MORE SUPPORT AND ADAPTATION FOR EARLY-ELEMENTARY STUDENTS.

NOTE

SEL Stories from Under the Sea

WELCOME TO THE UNDERWATER WORLD OF THE RAJA AMPAT REEF,
HOME TO AN AMAZING ARRAY OF SEA CREATURES AND MARINE LIFE!

Located in the western Pacific Ocean, off the coast of Indonesia, this reef is a vibrant ecosystem teeming with diversity, color, and wonder, much like the classrooms and learning environments we want all our children to inhabit. The reef and the sea life it nourishes are the inspiration for this collection of short stories and supporting activities.

Five tales, written in rhyme, highlight the life-long benefits children can enjoy when they develop and strengthen their social and emotional skills. With the help of lovable and charismatic characters – Daria Dugong, Duke Bottlenose Dolphin, Ollie Blue-Ringed Octopus, Muriel Manta Ray, and Shea Hawksbill Sea Turtle – the following skills are brought to life: **managing stress, using whole-body listening, resolving conflicts, expressing empathy**, and **making friends**.

How to Use the Activity Guide

Each skill is introduced in a story written to capture a child's attention and then supplemented by fun, engaging activities that support further skill development and academic growth. The activities allow children to explore art, movement, science and technology, writing, math, music, coloring, and structured group discussion.

You can blend the activities into existing academic lesson plans or subject areas, assign as homework, or teach as stand-alone lessons. Every activity features a list of materials, step-by-step teacher instructions, and any necessary supporting materials, such as worksheets and handouts.

The activities can be individualized or modified to accommodate the needs, capabilities, and learning styles of your students. The variety of options allows you to pick and choose multiple ways to help students enhance their understanding of a skill while growing academically. Some activities are specifically designed for collaboration and group work, while others can be done independently.

Storybook and Support Material PDFs

For your classroom, you can download a printable, full-color PDF student version of *Under the Sea*. All five stories, plus color photos and illustrations of the animals, are included, along with a helpful glossary highlighting words that may be new or unfamiliar to K-5 students. At the end of each story, a fun trivia question will test their knowledge about the marine animal. You can access PDFs of the storybook and additional support materials using the special code listed on the inside front cover of this guide.

Promote Social, Emotional, and Academic Growth

The stories combined with the activities focus on the social and emotional development kids need for greater success in school, in their relationships, and in life! As children acquire and expand their social-emotional skills, you can expect to see greater confidence, improved problem solving and decision making, more flexible thinking, and, best of all, engaged learners and empowered individuals.

As an added benefit, this material offers you an opportunity to introduce academic lessons or discussions about other important and timely topics, such as biodiversity, endangered species, marine ecosystems, or the impacts of climate change.

DUGONG

SKILL

DARIA, A DUGONG, IS A GENTLE GIANT WHO KNOWS HOW TO HANDLE STRESS AND ANXIETY. SHE TEACHES US, ALONG WITH THE SEA CREATURES, HOW TO OVERCOME WORRIES.

The name Daria means possessing goodness.

Daria Dugong was the calmest creature in the sea.
When the waters were rough, she remained as calm as could be.

The other creatures were always so full of fears.
They would fill the ocean with all of their tears.

Daria Dugong reassured them, "It's okay to cry.
But there are calm-down strategies you should try."

The creatures gave her a puzzled look,
but she knew she'd intrigued them with that hook.

Breathe in deeply to fill your body with air.
Then blow out slowly, five times, I dare.

Her dare was the hook they needed.
"Teach us more," they pleaded.

Q: Dugongs are sometimes referred to as what:
sea elephants/sea hippos/sea cows/ocean kittens

A: Sea Cows

Scan your body from head to toe.
Let the tension in your muscles go.

Build a castle in the sand.
Or listen to your favorite band.

Play a game or go for a swim.
Draw a picture or head for the gym.

Read your favorite book.
Or learn how to cook.

Go to your happy place.
Or imagine going into space.

Try them all until you find a few that work.
Have friends help you for an added perk.

No matter what you feel, you are never alone.
If you ever need help, call me on my shell phone.

Daria Dugong was one of the best teachers.
Her calm-down strategies worked for every creature.

They used the strategies when things got rough,
and they discovered they, too, are brave and tough.

Mindfulness Dugongs

MATERIALS

- "Dugong Drawing" worksheet
- Colored Pencils/Crayons/Markers

TEACHER INSTRUCTIONS

1. Distribute the "Dugong Drawing" worksheet.

2. Instruct students to draw an outline of a dugong.

3. Ask students to show and describe how they are feeling by filling in their dugong outline with colors, shapes, patterns, designs, and words that capture their current feelings and emotions.

4. Ask for volunteers to show and explain their drawings.

Name: ____ Date: __________________

Dugong Drawing

DIRECTIONS: Draw a large outline of a dugong, using a pencil, crayon, or marker. Then fill in your outline using colors, shapes, patterns, designs, or words that show the feelings and emotions you are experiencing today.

Daria Dugong Discussion Questions

MATERIALS

- Pencils
- "Discussion Questions" worksheet

TEACHER INSTRUCTIONS

1. Pass out the "Discussion Questions" worksheet.
2. Instruct students to fill out the worksheet by answering the questions.
3. Read the questions aloud and discuss possible answers as a group.

CLASS/GROUP DISCUSSION QUESTIONS

1. How many emotions can you name? List them:

2. Choose three emotions you listed for Question 1, then draw a picture of what you think each emotion looks like:

3. Does everyone feel emotions? Yes or No

4. Is it okay to feel every emotion? Why or why not?

5. While it's important to express emotions in appropriate, healthy ways, is it ever okay to hurt someone, something, or yourself when you feel angry? Yes or No

6. How can you express anger so you don't hurt someone, something, or yourself?

7. What does mindfulness mean to you?

8. What does it mean to use a calm-down strategy or coping skill? List as many calm-down strategies and coping skills as you can:

9. What calm-down strategies do you use to relax and calm your body?

10. Who are the trusted adults you can talk to about your emotions or go to if you need help calming down?

Name: ____   Date: _________________

Discussion Questions

DIRECTIONS: In the space provided, answer the questions. Be prepared to discuss your answers with the group.

1. How many emotions can you name? List them:______________________________________

____

2. Choose three emotions you listed for Question 1, then draw a picture of what you think each emotion looks like: 1.) ____

2.) ____

3.) ____

3. Does everyone feel emotions? *Yes or No*

4. Is it okay to feel every emotion? *Why or why not?* ___________________________________

____

____

Discussion Questions continued

5. While it's important to express emotions in appropriate, healthy ways, is it ever okay to hurt someone, something, or yourself when you feel angry? *Yes or No*

6. How can you express anger so you don't hurt someone, something, or yourself?________

____

____

____

7. What does mindfulness mean to you?____

____

8. What does it mean to use a calm-down strategy or coping skill? List as many calm-down strategies and coping skills as you can:____

____

____

____

____

9. What calm-down strategies do you use to relax and calm your body? ________________

____

____

10. Who are the trusted adults you can talk to about your emotions or go to if you need help calming down? ____

____

Mindful Breathing Like Daria Dugong

1. **Ask students the following question:** How can you practice mindful breathing like Daria?

    Demonstrate mindful breathing for students by breathing in deeply, then exhaling slowly, five times. Have students practice the technique, then ask the following questions:

    a. How do you feel?

    b. Do you feel more relaxed than you did before practicing your breathing?

2. **Say to the group:** Daria Dugong says, "Scan your body from head to toe. Let the tension in your muscles go."

    a. Ask students if they know how to scan their body, then demonstrate how to do it: Start with your head. Release your thoughts. Notice how your head and body feel in the moment. Take a deep breath in and slowly exhale. Roll your neck to the right and then to the left until you feel your neck muscles start to relax. Work your way down to your shoulders. Roll your shoulders forward and then backward. Now, shrug your shoulders up to your ears and back down again. Continue to pay attention to how your muscles feel. Take three deep breaths. Notice how your chest rises and falls with each breath. Wiggle your fingers. Now, clench your hands into a fist and release again. Do this a few times. Bend your right leg up and put it back down. Bend your left leg up and put it back down. Flex your feet up and down again. Wiggle your toes.

        Have students practice doing a body scan, then ask the following questions:
        - How did your body feel as you moved from your head to your toes?
        - How does your body feel now, after doing your body scan?

Drawing Activity

MATERIALS

- Color Paper/Poster Board
- "My Happy Place" poster
- "My Favorite Sea Creature Calms Down" poster
- "I Feel, I Do" poster
- "My Calm-Down Strategies" poster
- Colored Pencils/Crayons/Markers

TEACHER INSTRUCTIONS

1. Distribute the "My Happy Place," "My Favorite Sea Creature Calms Down," "I Feel, I Do," and "My Calm-Down Strategies" poster boards.

2. Review with students the directions for each poster.

3. Ask for volunteers to show and explain their drawings.

Name: ____ Date: _________________

My Happy Place Poster

DIRECTIONS: Draw a picture of your happy place, the place where you have the most fun or feel the most relaxed. Next to your picture, write down why it makes you feel so happy and relaxed.

Name: ____ Date: __________________

My Favorite Sea Creature Calms Down Poster

DIRECTIONS: Imagine your favorite sea creature is doing one of Daria's calm-down strategies, then draw a picture of what that looks like.

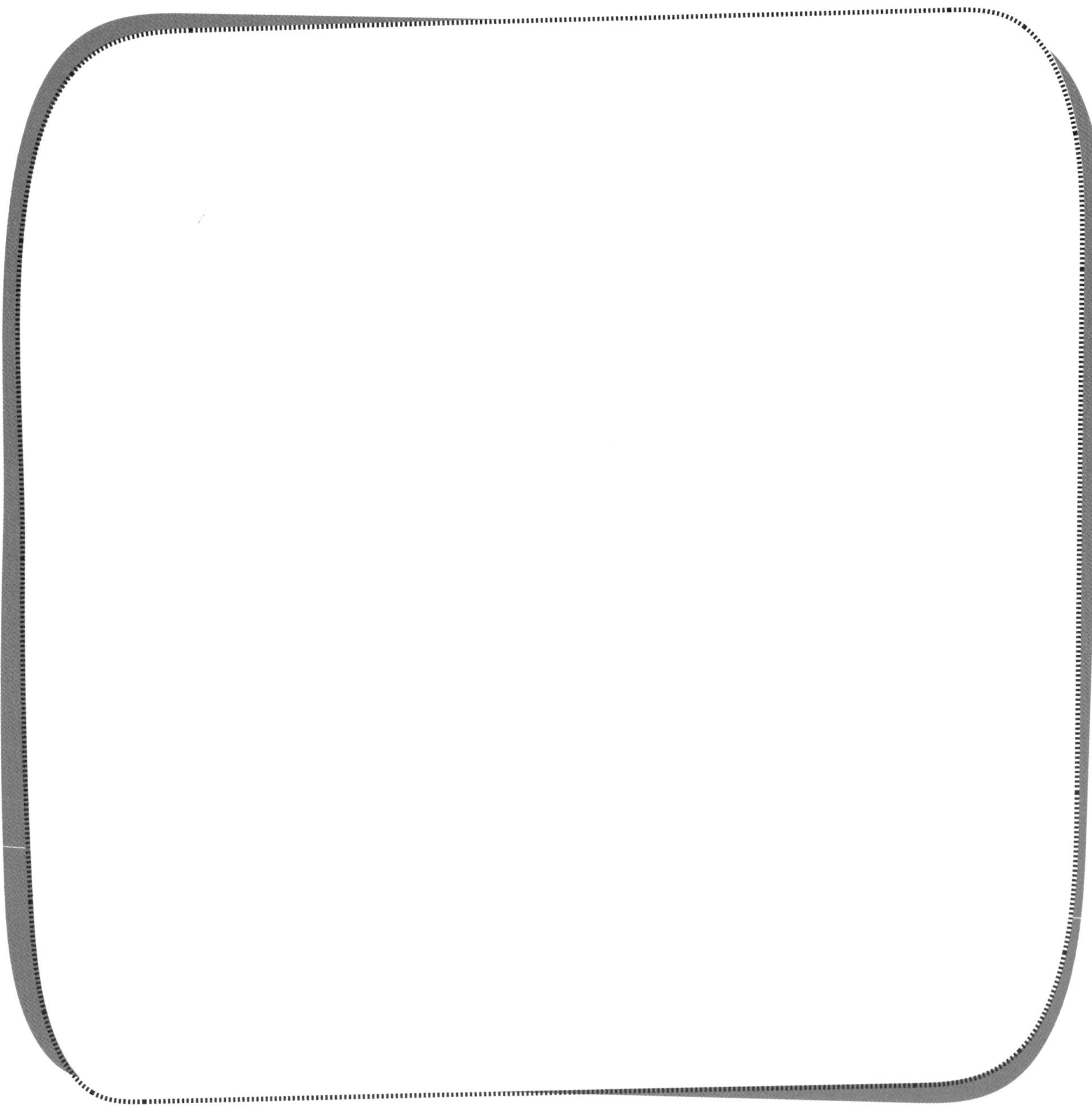

Name: ____   Date: _____________________

I Feel, I Do Poster

DIRECTIONS: Fold your paper or poster board in half. On the top half, draw three pictures that show three different emotions (happy, sad, angry, frustrated, bored, scared, nervous, surprised, embarrassed, etc.). On the bottom half, draw and label three calm-down strategies. You can choose strategies described in the story or others you know and have used.

Name: ____   Date: ___________________

My Calm-Down Strategies Poster

DIRECTIONS: Choose three calm-down strategies you would like to try, then draw a picture of yourself doing each one.

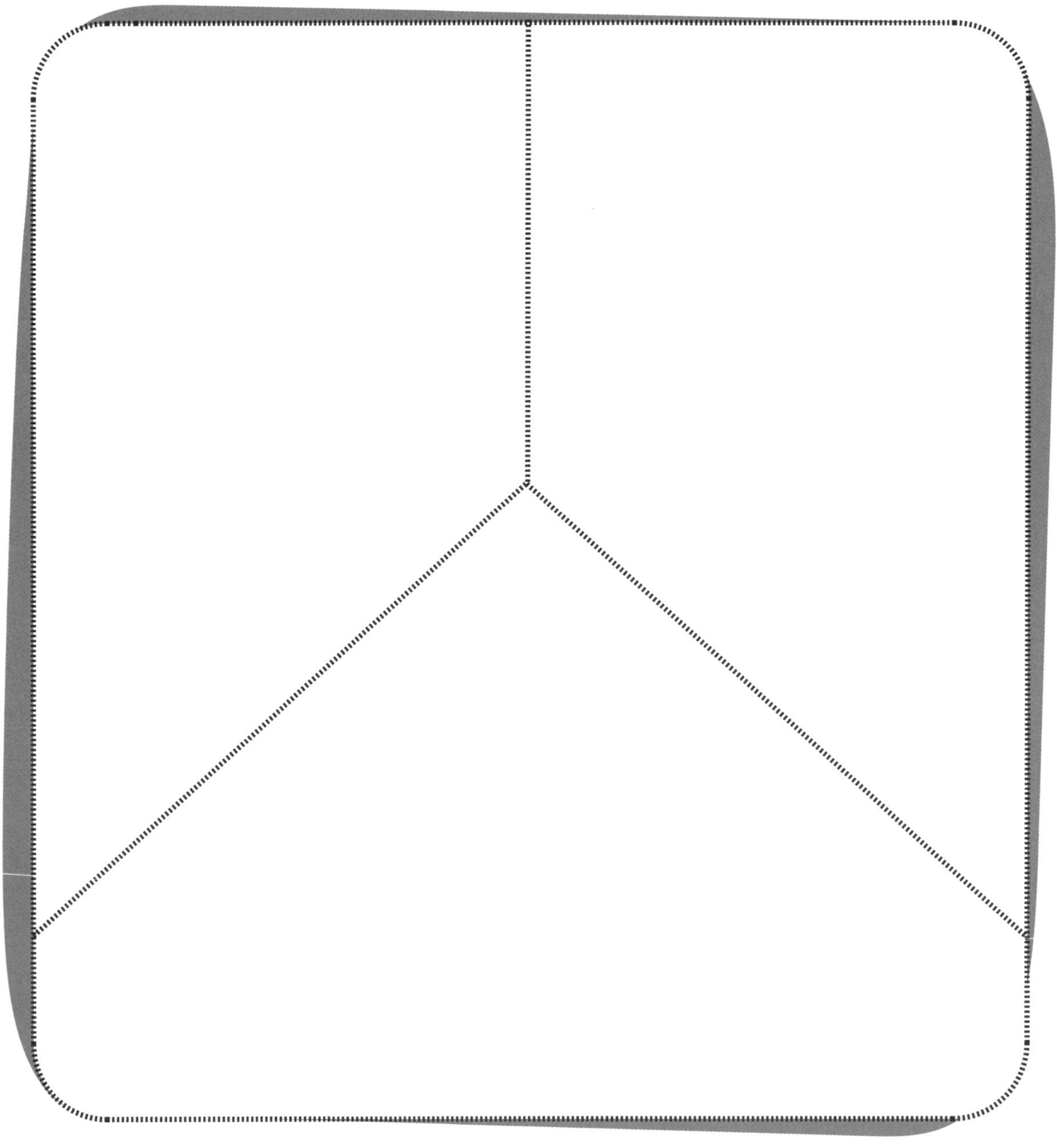

Math Activity

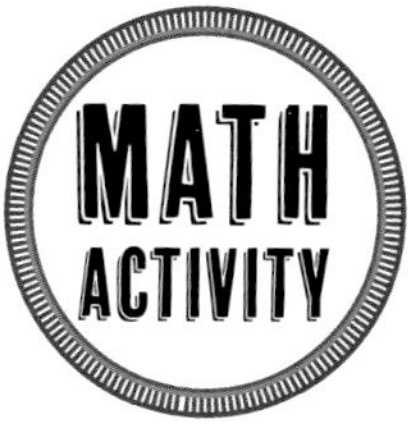

MATERIALS

- Pencils
- "Dugong Diet" worksheet

TEACHER INSTRUCTIONS

1. Hand out the "Dugong Diet" worksheet.

2. Allow at least 15 minutes for students to complete their worksheets.

3. Review answers as a class.

 You can add additional problems or edit the worksheet to include math skills or concepts most appropriate for your class or group.

Name: ____   Date: ____________________

Math Problems: Dugong Diet

DIRECTIONS: Answer each math problem and show your work by writing down all the steps you took to solve the problem.

FUN FACT: **Dugongs eat, on average, anywhere from 60 to 90 pounds of sea grass every day.**

1 If Daria eats 60 pounds of seagrass every day for seven days, how many pounds of seagrass will she have eaten at the end of one week?

2 If Daria eats 88 pounds of seagrass every day, how many pounds of seagrass will she eat in five days?

3 If Daria eats 85 pounds of seagrass on Sunday, 67 pounds of seagrass on Monday, 73 pounds of seagrass on Tuesday, 61 pounds of seagrass on Wednesday, 81 pounds of seagrass on Thursday, 63 pounds of seagrass on Friday, and 77 pounds of seagrass on Saturday, how many pounds of seagrass has she consumed?

4 During the first week of September, Daria ate 490 pounds of seagrass. The following week, Daria ate 595 pounds of seagrass. How many more pounds of seagrass did Daria eat during the second week of September?

Name: ___________________________ **ANSWER KEY** _______________ Date: ___________________

Math Problems: Dugong Diet

DIRECTIONS: Answer each math problem and show your work by writing down all the steps you took to solve the problem.

FUN FACT: Dugongs eat, on average, anywhere from 60 to 90 pounds of sea grass every day.

1 If Daria eats 60 pounds of seagrass every day for seven days, how many pounds of seagrass will she have eaten at the end of one week?

420
60x7=420
60+60+60+60+60+60+60=420

2 If Daria eats 88 pounds of seagrass every day, how many pounds of seagrass will she eat in five days?

440
88x5=440
88+88+88+88+88=440

3 If Daria eats 85 pounds of seagrass on Sunday, 67 pounds of seagrass on Monday, 73 pounds of seagrass on Tuesday, 61 pounds of seagrass on Wednesday, 81 pounds of seagrass on Thursday, 63 pounds of seagrass on Friday, and 77 pounds of seagrass on Saturday, how many pounds of seagrass has she consumed?

507
85+67+73+61+81+63+77=507

4 During the first week of September, Daria ate 490 pounds of seagrass. The following week, Daria ate 595 pounds of seagrass. How many more pounds of seagrass did Daria eat during the second week of September?

105
595-490=105

Nature Walk

Nature walks can be used as a calming strategy because walking helps release feel-good chemicals in the body. In addition, hiking allows you to explore and focus on the five senses (sight, sound, smell, touch, and taste), helping you feel more grounded and present in the moment.

MATERIALS

- "Things to Look for On My Nature Walk" worksheet
- Clipboard
- Lined/Ruled Paper
- Pencils

TEACHER INSTRUCTIONS

1. Pass out the "Things to Look for On My Nature Walk" worksheet.

2. Lead a nature walk and have students look for the following items:

THINGS TO LOOK FOR ON OUR NATURE WALK

☐ Leaf	☐ Rock	☐ Something Yellow
☐ Stick	☐ Ant	☐ Something Green
☐ Acorn	☐ Flying Bug	☐ Something Brown
☐ Bird	☐ Insect	☐ Something Blue
☐ Squirrel	☐ Pinecone	☐ Something Smooth
☐ Cloud	☐ Sign	☐ Something Rough
☐ Tree	☐ Something Red	☐ Something Circular
☐ Flower		

Name: ____ Date: _____________________

Things to Look for On My Nature Walk

DIRECTIONS: Can you find all these items on your nature walk? Put an X next to each item you spot and include a description (size, appearance, color, feel, location, smell, etc.).

- ☐ Leaf ____
- ☐ Stick ____
- ☐ Acorn ____
- ☐ Bird ____
- ☐ Squirrel ____
- ☐ Cloud ____
- ☐ Tree ____
- ☐ Flower ____
- ☐ Rock ____
- ☐ Ant ____
- ☐ Flying Bug ____
- ☐ Insect ____
- ☐ Pinecone ____
- ☐ Sign ____
- ☐ Something Red ____
- ☐ Something Yellow _______________________________________
- ☐ Something Green ____
- ☐ Something Brown _______________________________________
- ☐ Something Blue ____
- ☐ Something Smooth ______________________________________
- ☐ Something Rough _______________________________________
- ☐ Something Circular _____________________________________

Calm Music, Calm Mood

MATERIALS

- "Calm Music, Calm Mood" handout
- Paper
- Pencils
- Device with internet access

TEACHER INSTRUCTIONS

1. Distribute the "Calm Music, Calm Mood" handout.

2. Instruct students to write down three to five (or five to ten) song titles/lyrics/musicians they listen to when they want to relax or calm down.

3. Share with students your go-to songs/lyrics/musicians when you want to relax.

4. Provide time for students to research songs/lyrics/musicians if they need help creating their lists.

Name: ____   Date: ___________________

Calm Music, Calm Mood

DIRECTIONS: Write down the song titles, lyrics, or musicians you listen to when you want to calm down and relax.

1 _______________________________

____

____

2 _______________________________

____

____

3 _______________________________

____

____

4 _______________________________

____

____

5 _______________________________

____

____

6 _______________________________

____

____

7 _______________________________

____

____

8 _______________________________

____

____

9 _______________________________

____

____

10 _______________________________

____

____

Science Activity

MATERIALS

- "Dugong Research Notes" worksheet
- Pencils

TEACHER INSTRUCTIONS

1. Distribute the "Dugong Research Notes" worksheet to students.

2. Instruct students to use classroom and online research tools to gather facts and information about dugongs. Then ask them to write a short essay summarizing their research findings. Encourage students to follow the outline provided on their worksheets when writing their essays.

3. Ask for volunteers to read their essays aloud.

Name: ____   Date: ____________________

Dugong Research Notes

DIRECTIONS: Use classroom resources and websites to learn facts and information about dugongs. Write down your findings in the appropriate boxes, then use that information to write a five-paragraph essay about this marine mammal.

1 **Paragraph 1:** Introduction

2 **Paragraph 2:** Appearance

3 **Paragraph 3:** Habitat and Diet

4 **Paragraph 4:** Interesting Facts

5 **Paragraph 5:** Conclusion

Fun Facts about Dugongs

MATERIALS

- "Fun Facts about Dugongs" worksheet
- Computer/Laptop
- Internet access

TEACHER INSTRUCTIONS

1. Pass out the "Fun Facts about Dugongs" worksheet.

2. Ask students to research fun and interesting facts about dugongs and answer the following questions:

1. How can you estimate a dugong's age?

2. How long can a dugong hold its breath?

3. What is the closest land relative to the dugong?

4. How long can a dugong live?

5. How much does an average dugong weigh?

6. What other interesting facts did you discover?

3. Have students create a slideshow or video presentation that highlights the answers to each question and any other information students learned. Ask for volunteers to share their slideshows and videos with the class.

 Do this activity in small groups of two, three, or four students.

Name: ____   Date: ___________________

Fun Facts about Dugongs

DIRECTIONS: Research facts about dugongs and then answer the questions below. Use the answers and any other information you learn to create a slideshow or video presentation.

1. How can you estimate a dugong's age?____

____

____

2. How long can a dugong hold its breath? _______________________________________

____

____

3. What is the closest land relative to the dugong?________________________________

____

____

4. How long can a dugong live? ____

____

____

5. How much does an average dugong weigh? ____________________________________

____

____

6. What other interesting facts did you discover? _________________________________

____

____

____

____

____

Writing Activities

MATERIALS

- "Vocabulary Words" worksheet
- "Describe the Picture" worksheet
- "Finish the Sentence" worksheet
- "Should We Practice Calm-Down Strategies Every Morning in the Classroom?" worksheet
- "When I'm Worried" worksheet
- Pencils

TEACHER INSTRUCTIONS

1. Pass out all five worksheets for students to complete at one time, or have them complete one worksheet per day during the school week.

2. Instruct students to fill out their worksheets and be prepared to discuss their answers as a group.

3. Allow enough time for students to complete the writing activity, then review and discuss the assignment as a group.

Name: ____ Date: ___________________

Vocabulary Words

DIRECTIONS: Write original sentences that include the vocabulary words listed below. Each word needs to be used at least once, and a sentence can have more than one vocabulary word in it. When all the words have been used in sentences, draw a comic strip or a picture that represents or reflects as many of the vocabulary words as possible.

Vocabulary Words: Fear, Calm-Down Strategies, Try, Breathe, Teach, Body, Happy, Friend, Feel, Discover

Name: ____   Date: ___________________

Describe the Picture

DIRECTIONS: Look at the picture and then fill in the worksheet.

1. This is a picture of what? ____

____

2. What is happening in the picture? ____

____

____

3. Where do you think this picture was taken (setting/location)? ___________________

____

____

4. Write an original sentence that includes your answers to the questions above: _________

____

____

____

____

____

____

____

____

____

____

____

Name: ____ Date: ___________________

Finish the Sentence

DIRECTIONS: Complete the sentence and then draw a picture to match your sentence.

I CAN CALM DOWN BY ____

____

____

____

____

____

Name: ____ Date: ___________________

Should We Practice Calm-Down Strategies Every Morning in the Classroom?

DIRECTIONS: Fill in the worksheet by answering yes or no if you think our class should practice calm-down strategies every morning. Write down three reasons to support your answer.

Should our class practice calm-down strategies every morning?

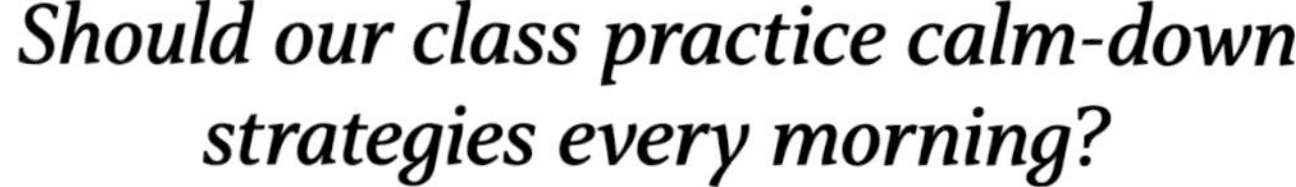

REASON   REASON   REASON

Name: ____   Date: ___________________

When I'm Worried

DIRECTIONS: Read the text and then answer the questions.

TEXT: Think about a time when you felt really worried, such as when your parents were late picking you up, or when you were about to take a big test, or before your first competition.

1. What were you worried about? ___________________________________
   ____

2. What did your body feel like? ___________________________________
   ____
   ____

3. What, if anything, did you do to calm yourself? __________________
   ____
   ____

4. What will you do the next time you feel worried? _________________
   ____
   ____
   ____
   ____

NOTES

BOTTLENOSE DOLPHIN

SKILL

DUKE, A BOTTLENOSE DOLPHIN, IS AN EXCELLENT LISTENER WHO SHOWS US HOW TO USE WHOLE-BODY LISTENING.

The name Duke means leader.

Duke Dolphin is the best listener in the whole sea.
When others talk, he remains as quiet as can be.

He likes to use whole-body listening,
which starts with his body's positioning.

Duke turns his body to the sea creature who's about to speak,
and makes sure not a single sound slips through his stubby beak.

He looks the speaker in the eyes to show he's paying attention.
He uses his ears to listen while his brain works hard on retention.

His flippers stay motionless by his sides,
even with the rise and fall of the tides.

Good listening helps show he has a caring heart.
Sometimes, it even helps him earn stickers on his chart.

Q: Do bottlenose dolphins chew their food, and what kind of food do they eat?

A: No! Fish, Shrimp, Crabs, Squid, and Crustaceans

Duke likes to be a role model to all the sea creatures,
showing them how to leave a positive impression on their teachers.

He reminds every creature to follow directions,
so they won't have to make any corrections.

Whole-body listening is important if you want to succeed.
It's a life-long skill every leader needs.

Art Activity

MATERIALS

- "Directed Drawing" worksheet
- Pencils

TEACHER INSTRUCTIONS

1. Hand out the "Directed Drawing" worksheet.

2. Explain to students that this activity will test their listening skills. Ask them to draw a picture based on the verbal instructions you give them.

3. Read the first instruction aloud, then allow time for students to draw. Read aloud the next instruction and so on until all the instructions or steps have been said aloud.

4. When finished, ask for volunteers to show their drawings to the group.

DIRECTED DRAWING: Verbal Instructions to Students

STEP 1 Divide your paper into three sections. The sections do not have to be equal size.

STEP 2 Color the top section of your paper light blue. This will be the background for your sky.

STEP 3 Draw a bright yellow sun.

STEP 4 Draw two clouds.

STEP 5 The rest of your paper is going to be the ocean. Color the ocean dark blue.

STEP 6 Draw big waves.

STEP 7 Draw three things in your ocean. Things can include seashells, animals, boats, swimmers, or anything you might see in the ocean.

Name: ____   Date: __________________

Directed Drawing

DIRECTIONS: This activity will test your listening skills. Draw a picture based on the verbal instructions you hear.

Duke Bottlenose Dolphin
Discussion Questions

MATERIALS

- Pencils
- "Discussion Questions" worksheet

TEACHER INSTRUCTIONS

1. Pass out the "Discussion Questions" worksheet.

2. Instruct students to complete the worksheet by answering the questions.

3. Read the questions aloud and discuss possible answers as a group.

CLASS/GROUP DISCUSSION QUESTIONS

1. What does it mean to be a good listener?

2. What does whole-body listening look like?

3. What happens when you or a classmate are not listening?

4. How does it make you feel when you are talking to others, and they are not paying attention?

5. How do you think others feel when they try to talk to you, but you do not pay attention?

6. How do you think your classmates feel when you create distractions while they are trying to pay attention?

7. How would you feel if you were trying to pay attention and someone else was creating distractions?

8. Why is it important to follow directions?

9. What happens if you do not follow directions at school?

10. What happens if you do not follow directions at home?

Name: ____   Date: ____________________

Discussion Questions

DIRECTIONS: In the space provided, answer the following questions. Be prepared to discuss your answers with the group.

1. What does it mean to be a good listener? ____

____

____

____

2. What does whole-body listening look like? _______________________________________

____

____

____

3. What happens when you or a classmate are not listening? ___________________________

____

____

____

4. How does it make you feel when you are talking to others, and they are not paying

attention? ____

____

____

____

5. How do you think others feel when they try to talk to you, but you do not pay attention?

____

____

____

____

6. How do you think your classmates feel when you create distractions while they are trying to pay attention? ____

____

____

7. How would you feel if you were trying to pay attention and someone else was creating distractions? ____

____

____

8. Why is it important to follow directions? ____

____

____

9. What happens if you do not follow directions at school? ____

____

____

10. What happens if you do not follow directions at home? ____

____

____

Drawing Activity

MATERIALS

- "Whole-Body Listening" Paper/Poster Board
- Colored Pencils/Crayons/Markers

TEACHER INSTRUCTIONS

1. Distribute the "Whole-Body Listening" paper/poster board.

2. Review with students the directions for the poster.

3. Ask for volunteers to show and explain their drawings.

Name: ____   Date: ___________________

Whole-Body Listening Poster

DIRECTIONS: Draw a picture of what your body looks like when you practice or do whole-body listening. Label the parts of the body (arms/hands, legs/feet, mouth, eyes, ears, brain, etc.) and write down what each part does during whole-body listening.

Math Activity

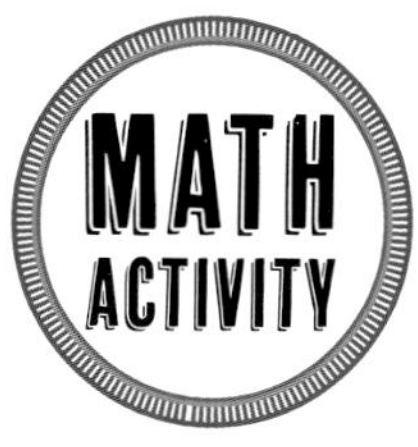

MATERIALS

- Chalk/Tape

TEACHER INSTRUCTIONS

1. Use chalk or tape to draw a calculator on the floor (or wall) that looks like this ⟶

7	8	9	-
4	5	6	+
1	2	3	=
x	÷	0	

2. Give students a math problem and then have them step (or tap) on the appropriate squares to calculate the correct answer. For example, if you ask them to find the answer to 1 plus 2, students should step or tap on 1, then step or tap on the plus symbol, then step or tap on 2, then step or tap on the equal sign, and then step or tap on 3.

3. Use age- and skill-appropriate math problems that also incorporate dolphins and whole-body listening. Here are two examples:

- 2 listening dolphins + 2 listening dolphins = how many listening dolphins?

- If 25 dolphins are in class but only 18 use whole-body listening, how many dolphins are not listening?

Movement Activity

MATERIALS

- Hula Hoops
- Soft Foam Balls

TEACHER INSTRUCTIONS

1. Have students do three movement exercises. Start **Exercise 1** by telling the class: Dolphins are talented creatures. Have you ever seen them perform in dolphin shows? These performances often involve dolphins jumping through hula hoops or spinning them on their beaks.

2. Group students into pairs. Instruct one student to gently toss a hula hoop in the air, and have their partner try to catch it with their foot (or arm or neck). Students should count how many successful tosses/catches they can do in a row. After five minutes, have the partners switch roles and repeat the exercise.

3. **Exercise 2:** Have students try to spin a hula hoop around their necks. When they master spinning one hula hoop, have them add a second hula hoop and so on to see how many hula hoops they can spin at once.

4. **Exercise 3:** Group students into pairs. Instruct one student to gently toss a foam ball at their partner, who then must try to hit it back using only their head. The partners will continue batting the ball back and forth using only their heads.

For students with limited mobility or related health issues, consider modifying the activities to best accommodate their needs.

Follow the Leader: Dance Edition

MATERIALS

- Music (optional)

TEACHER INSTRUCTIONS

1. Divide the class into groups of three or four.

2. Instruct each group to pick a leader.

3. Give the group leaders five to ten minutes to create a dance, and then have them teach the dance to their group members.

4. Encourage group members to listen closely and pay attention to the group leader so they can do the dance exactly how their leader described it to them.

 Have music playing in the background to add to the fun!

Science Activity

MATERIALS

- "Bottlenose Dolphin Research Notes" worksheet
- Pencils

TEACHER INSTRUCTIONS

1. Distribute the "Bottlenose Dolphin Research Notes" worksheet.

2. Instruct students to use classroom and online research tools to gather facts and information about bottlenose dolphins. Then ask them to write a short essay summarizing their research findings. Encourage students to follow the outline provided on their worksheets when writing their essays.

3. Ask for volunteers to read their essays aloud.

Name: ____   Date: __________________

Bottlenose Dolphin Research Notes

DIRECTIONS: Use classroom resources and websites to learn facts and information about bottlenose dolphins. Write down your findings in the appropriate boxes, then use that information to write a five-paragraph essay about this marine mammal.

1 Paragraph 1: Introduction

2 Paragraph 2: Appearance

3 Paragraph 3: Habitat and Diet

4 Paragraph 4: Interesting Facts

5 Paragraph 5: Conclusion

How Do Dolphins Sleep?

MATERIALS

- "Sleeping Habits of Dolphins" worksheet
- Computer/Laptop
- Internet access

TEACHER INSTRUCTIONS

1. Pass out the "Sleeping Habits of Dolphins" worksheet.

2. Ask students to research the sleeping habits of dolphins and answer the following questions:

    1. How do dolphins sleep?

    2. How long do dolphins sleep?

    3. Do dolphins close their eyes when sleeping?

    4. Are dolphins unconscious or unaware when sleeping?

    5. Do dolphins' vision and hearing become inactive when they're sleeping?

    6. What other interesting facts did you discover?

3. Have students create a slideshow or video presentation that highlights the answers to each question and any other information students learned. Ask for volunteers to share their slideshows and videos with the class.

Do this activity in small groups of two, three, or four students.

Name: ____   Date: __________________

Sleeping Habits of Dolphins

DIRECTIONS: Research how dolphins sleep and then answer the questions below. Use the answers and any other information you learn to create a slideshow or video presentation.

1. How do dolphins sleep? ____

____

____

2. How long do dolphins sleep? ____

____

____

3. Do dolphins close their eyes when sleeping? ________________________________

____

____

4. Are dolphins unconscious or unaware when sleeping? ________________________

____

____

5. Do dolphins' vision and hearing become inactive when they're sleeping?____________

____

____

6. What other interesting facts did you discover? ________________________________

____

____

____

____

Writing Activities

MATERIALS

- "Vocabulary Words" worksheet
- "Describe the Picture" worksheet
- "Finish the Sentence" worksheet
- "Should We Practice Whole-Body Listening Every Morning in the Classroom?" worksheet
- "No One Is Listening to Me" worksheet
- Pencils

TEACHER INSTRUCTIONS

1. Pass out all five worksheets for students to complete at one time, or have them complete one worksheet per day during the school week.

2. Instruct students to fill out their worksheets and be prepared to discuss their answers as a group.

3. Allow enough time for students to complete the writing activity, then review and discuss the assignment as a group.

Name: ____   Date: _____________________

Vocabulary Words

DIRECTIONS: Write original sentences that include the vocabulary words listed below. Each word needs to be used at least once, and a sentence can have more than one vocabulary word in it. When all the words have been used in sentences, draw a comic strip or a picture that represents or reflects as many of the vocabulary words as possible.

Vocabulary Words: Talk, Quiet, Whole-Body Listening, Body, Eyes, Ears, Listen, Heart, Teacher, Directions

Name: ____   Date: _____________________

Describe the Picture Worksheet

DIRECTIONS: Look at the picture and then fill in the worksheet.

1. This is a picture of what? ____

    ____

2. What is happening in the picture? ____

    ____

    ____

3. Where do you think this picture was taken (setting/location)? ______________________

    ____

    ____

4. Write an original sentence that includes your answers to the questions above: _________

    ____

    ____

    ____

    ____

    ____

    ____

    ____

    ____

    ____

    ____

    ____

Name: ____ Date: ___________________

Finish the Sentence

DIRECTIONS: Complete the sentence and then draw a picture to match your sentence.

I CAN SHOW MY TEACHER I AM LISTENING BY_____________________________

____

____

____

____

Name: ____   Date: __________________

Should We Practice Whole-Body Listening Every Morning in the Classroom?

DIRECTIONS: Fill in the worksheet by answering yes or no if you think our class should practice whole-body listening every morning. Write down three reasons to support your answer.

Should our class practice whole-body listening every morning?

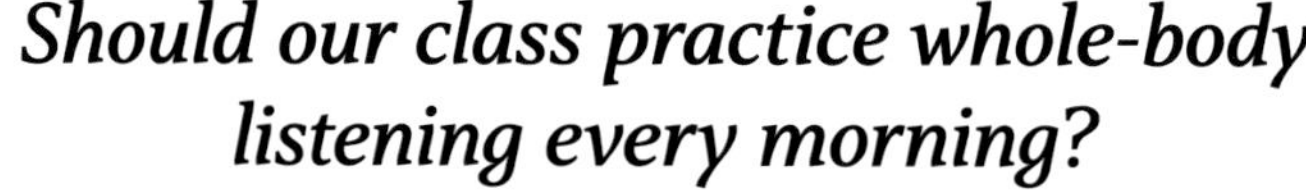

REASON   REASON   REASON

Name: ____   Date: ____________________

No One Is Listening to Me

DIRECTIONS: Read the text and then answer the questions.

TEXT: Think about a time when you were excited to talk to someone, such as a grandparent, a teacher, or a friend, and they didn't really listen or pay attention to you.

1. What did you want to tell that person? _______________________________________

   ____

2. How did you feel **before** you started talking to them?_____________________________

   ____

   ____

3. How did you feel when the person wasn't listening? _________________________________

   ____

   ____

4. How would you have felt if the person had paid more attention and listened to you?

   ____

   ____

   ____

   ____

   ____

   ____

NOTES

BLUE-RINGED OCTOPUS

SKILL

OLLIE, A BLUE-RINGED OCTOPUS, USED TO GET REALLY ANGRY AT THE OTHER SEA CREATURES AND BULLY THEM IF SHE DIDN'T GET HER WAY. ONE DAY, SHE WAS CAUGHT AND FACED A CONSEQUENCE. HER PUNISHMENT WAS TO GO AROUND TEACHING YOUNGER SEA CREATURES HOW TO PEACEFULLY SOLVE PROBLEMS USING I-STATEMENTS. THIS BLUE-RINGED OCTOPUS TEACHES US HOW TO PROBLEM SOLVE.

The name Ollie means olive tree, a symbol of peace.

Ollie Octopus was full of rage.
She was a bully from a young age.

When she did not get her way,
she had nothing nice to say.

She called other kids mean names,
and her body filled up with flames.

Her face turned bright red,
and pain filled her head.

Her stomach would ache,
and her body would shake.

Her hearts would beat really fast.
She looked like she was going to blast.

Whenever Ollie began to sweat,
you knew you should start to fret.

Ollie Octopus clenched her jaw,
looking for young sea creatures to gnaw.

Ollie shoved, kicked, hit, and tripped.
And then held them down with a tight grip.

She threatened them until they cried.
She made everyone want to hide.

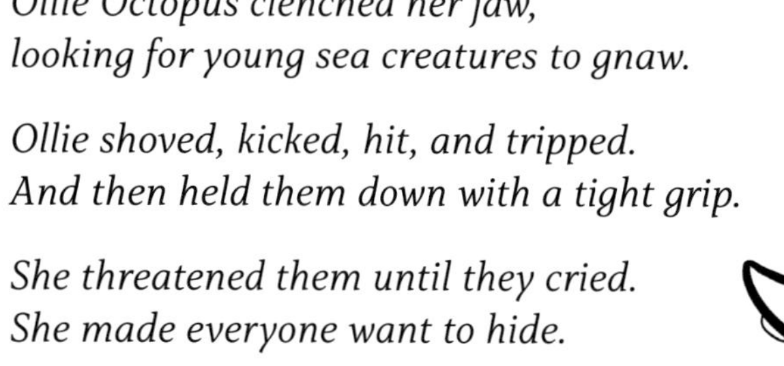

One day, Ollie got caught being a bully.
So the teacher made her apologize fully.

Ollie Octopus was stopped in her tracks,
and she was punished for her horrible acts.

She needed to teach the younger creatures to solve problems in a peaceful way,
so all of them could feel positive emotions instead of feeling gray.

Ollie said using I-statements lets others know how you feel.
It helps you to communicate and work out a deal.

If someone takes your toy,
you could say to the boy:

I feel angry when you take my toys and don't ask,
next time, could you please remember that simple task?

If someone calls you a name,
you should definitely proclaim:

I feel upset when you call me fat,
could you please stop using words like that?

If someone pushes you,
and makes you feel blue...

You could look at them and say:
I felt blue when you pushed me today.

Please don't ever push me,
or hurt me to such a degree.

Ollie Octopus taught problem-solving and I-statement lessons to everyone.
She wanted to make all their relationships more loving, positive, and fun.

Problem solving is an important skill to have in life.
It can help you avoid major strife.

Positive communication also will help you grow,
and develop those life-long friendships that make you glow.

Under the Sea Building Challenge

MATERIALS

- Building Blocks/Bricks
- "Build an Octopus" worksheet
- Scissors
- Tape/Glue

TEACHER INSTRUCTIONS

1. Divide the class into groups of three or four.

2. Instruct each group to build an underwater seascape that includes an octopus.

3. Encourage the groups to include other sea creatures in their designs.

4. Ask each group to show and explain their creations to the class.

5. Have students practice saying I-statements using the octopus and the other sea creatures they created.

6. Allow students to vote for their favorite seascape.

Hand out the "Build an Octopus" worksheet to each student. Have them write an I-statement on each of the arms. Then instruct them to cut out the arms and other body parts and paste them together.

Name: ____   Date: ___________________

Build an Octopus

DIRECTIONS: Write an I-statement on each arm, then cut out and paste the arms and head together to make an octopus. If you need help writing I-statements, go back and read the Ollie Octopus story for examples.

Ollie Blue-Ringed Octopus
Discussion Questions

MATERIALS

- Pencils
- "Discussion Questions" worksheet

TEACHER INSTRUCTIONS

1. Pass out the "Discussion Questions" worksheet.

2. Instruct students to fill out the worksheet by answering the questions.

3. Read the questions aloud and discuss possible answers as a group.

CLASS/GROUP DISCUSSION QUESTIONS

1. What is bullying?
   *[*Answer: Repeated acts of aggression or harm by individuals who have more power than their victims.]*

2. How does your body express or feel anger (red face, tummy ache, sweating, shaking, rapid heartbeat, etc.)?

3. What does it mean to threaten someone?

4. Is it okay to threaten someone?

5. Why is it important to solve problems peacefully?

6. What is an I-statement?

7. Write down three examples of I-statements:
   [Answers can include: I feel angry when someone takes my pencil; I feel sad when someone says mean things to me; I feel upset when someone cuts in front of me.]

* Reference: Handwerk, M. (2005). Defining the problem. In J. Bolton & S. Graeve (Eds.), **No Room for Bullies** (p. 9). Boys Town, NE: Boys Town Press.

Name: ____ Date: ___________________

Discussion Worksheet

DIRECTIONS: In the space provided, answer the following questions. Be prepared to discuss your answers with the group.

1. What is bullying? ____

   ____

   ____

2. How does your body express or feel anger (red face, tummy ache, sweating, shaking, rapid heartbeat, etc.)? ____

   ____

3. What does it mean to threaten someone? _____________________________________

   ____

   ____

4. Is it okay to threaten someone? ____

   ____

5. Why is it important to solve problems peacefully? ______________________________

   ____

   ____

6. What is an I-statement? ____

   ____

   ____

7. Write down three examples of I-statements:

   1. ____

   2. ____

   3. ____

Drawing Activity

MATERIALS

- Paper/Poster Board
- "What My Anger Looks Like" poster
- "I-Statement" poster
- Colored Pencils/Crayons/Markers

TEACHER INSTRUCTIONS

1. Distribute the "What My Anger Looks Like" and "I-Statement" poster papers.

2. Review with students the directions for each poster.

3. Ask for volunteers to show and explain their drawings.

Name: ____ Date: ___________________

What My Anger Looks Like Poster

DIRECTIONS: Draw a picture of your body when it feels and shows anger. Label each part of your body (arms/hands, legs/feet, mouth, eyes, ears, head, etc.), including how it feels and what it does when you are angry.

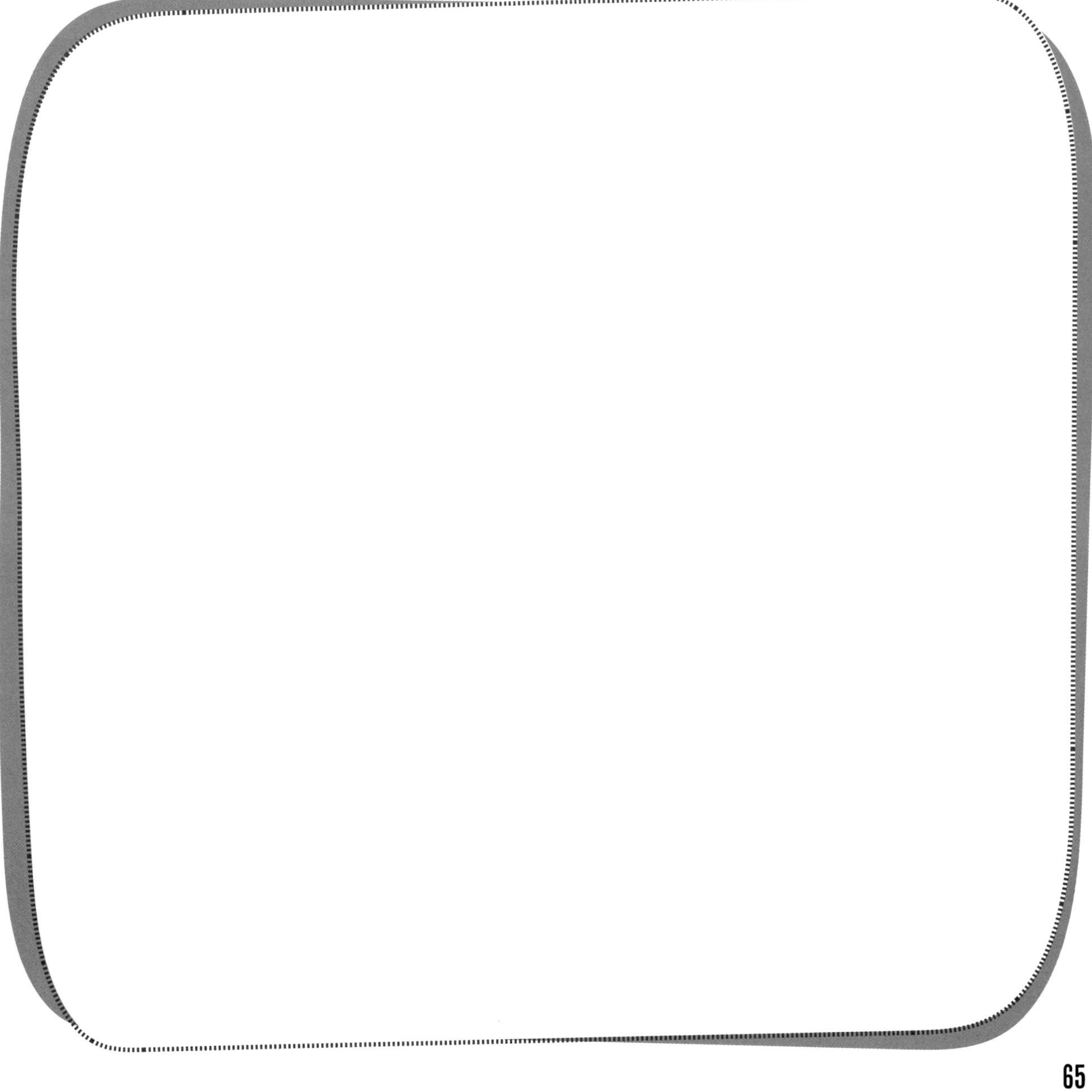

Name: ____   Date: __________________

I-Statement Poster

DIRECTIONS: Draw a picture showing a scene or situation where someone uses an I-statement. Write the I-statement on your poster.

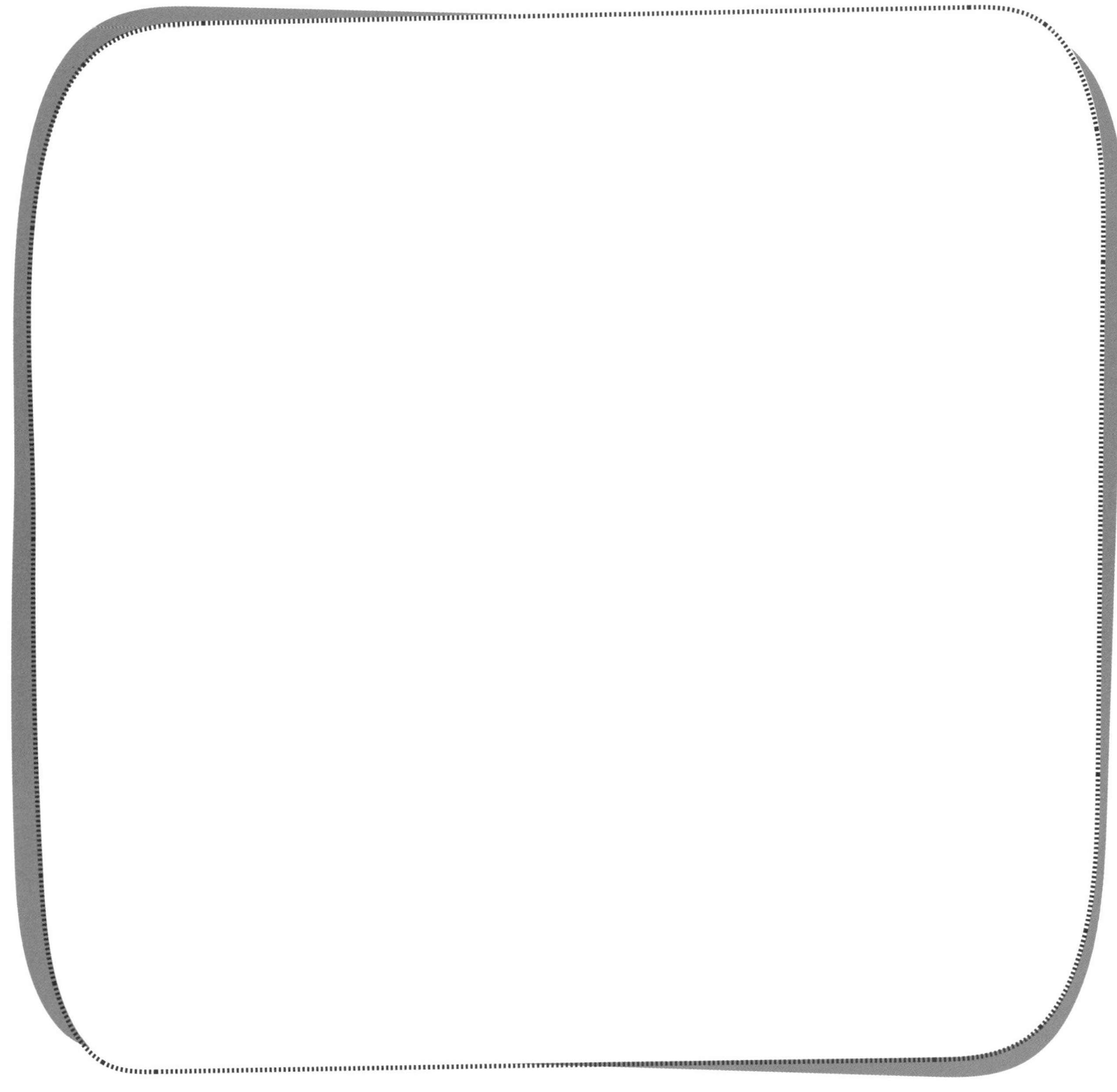

Math Activity

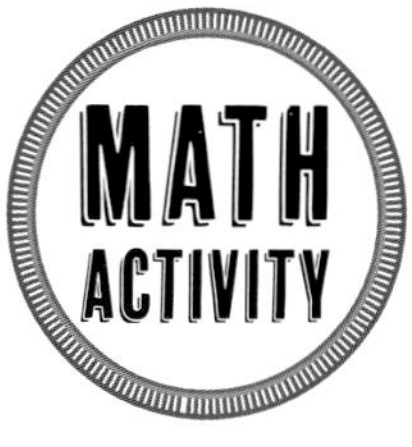

MATERIALS

- Pencils
- "Ollie Octopus" worksheet

TEACHER INSTRUCTIONS

1. Hand out the "Ollie Octopus" worksheet.

2. Allow at least 15 minutes for students to complete their worksheets.

3. Review answers as a class.

 Use the blank "Ollie Octopus" worksheet to add math problems tailored to your students' skill level.

Name: ____   Date: ___________________

Math Problems: Ollie Octopus

DIRECTIONS: Answer each math problem and show your work by writing down all the steps you took to solve the problem.

Ollie is carrying blue and green crayons in three arms. She holds 13 green crayons in one arm. Her second arm holds 13 blue crayons. Her third arm holds 6 blue crayons and 7 green crayons. If Ollie drops 6 blue crayons and 10 green crayons, how many blue crayons is she still holding? How many green crayons is she still holding? How many green and blue crayons is she still holding?

Name: ___________________________ **ANSWER KEY** ___________________________   Date: ___________________

Math Problems: Ollie Octopus

DIRECTIONS: Answer each math problem and show your work by writing down all the steps you took to solve the problem.

Ollie is carrying blue and green crayons in three arms. She holds 13 green crayons in one arm. Her second arm holds 13 blue crayons. Her third arm holds 6 blue crayons and 7 green crayons. If Ollie drops 6 blue crayons and 10 green crayons, how many blue crayons is she still holding? How many green crayons is she still holding? How many green and blue crayons is she still holding?

Blue Crayons = 13   Green Crayons = 10   Blue and Green Crayons = 23

Name: ____   Date: __________________

Math Problems: Ollie Octopus

DIRECTIONS: Answer each math problem and show your work by writing down all the steps you took to solve the problem.

Octopus Tag

MATERIALS

- Gym/Play Area

TEACHER INSTRUCTIONS

1. Ask students to line up on one side of the gym or play area.

2. Designate one student to play the role of the octopus. That student will stand in the middle of the gym or play area and yell "Go!" when instructed.

3. When the octopus yells "Go!," students (players) will attempt to run across the gym or play area to get to the other side while the octopus tries to tag them. Any players the octopus tags must freeze in place. Players that make it to the other side without being tagged are safe. Repeat the process again, with the octopus yelling "Go!" and the remaining players running across the gym or play area. Any players who were tagged in the first round should remain standing in place, but they can help the octopus by reaching their arms out and tagging any players running by them.

4. When everyone gets tagged, the game ends. Play again and designate a different student to be the octopus.

Create An Anti-Bullying Anthem

MATERIALS

- "Anti-Bullying" song sheet
- Paper
- Pencils

TEACHER INSTRUCTIONS

1. Divide the class into small groups or pairs.

2. Ask each group to write lyrics for an anti-bullying song, then distribute the song sheet handout to the groups.

3. Ask for volunteers to share their lyrics or perform their song for the whole class.

Name: ____   Date: __________________

Anti-Bullying Song Sheet

DIRECTIONS: Create and write lyrics for an anti-bullying song. Your song should have at least two stanzas, each four lines long. Use rhyme or repetition to create a memorable song! Be prepared to sing or rap the song for the class!

MY ANTI-BULLYING SONG

____

____

____

____

____

____

____

____

____

____

____

____

Science Activity

MATERIALS

- "Blue-Ringed Octopus Research Notes" worksheet
- Pencils

TEACHER INSTRUCTIONS

1. Distribute the "Blue-Ringed Octopus Research Notes" worksheet to students.

2. Instruct students to use classroom and online research tools to gather facts and information about the blue-ringed octopus. Then ask them to write a short essay summarizing their research findings. Encourage students to follow the outline provided on their worksheets when writing their essays.

3. Ask for volunteers to read their essays aloud.

Name: ____   Date: _____________________

Blue-Ringed Octopus Research Notes Worksheet

DIRECTIONS: Use classroom resources and websites to learn facts and information about the blue-ringed octopus. Write down your findings in the appropriate boxes, then use that information to write a five-paragraph essay about this special sea creature.

1 **Paragraph 1:** Introduction

2 **Paragraph 2:** Appearance

3 **Paragraph 3:** Habitat and Diet

4 **Paragraph 4:** Interesting Facts

5 **Paragraph 5:** Conclusion

Life Cycle of the Blue-Ringed Octopus

MATERIALS

- "Life Cycle of the Blue-Ringed Octopus" worksheet
- Computer/Laptop
- Internet access

TEACHER INSTRUCTIONS

1. Pass out the "Life Cycle of the Blue-Ringed Octopus" worksheet.

2. Ask students to research the blue-ringed octopus life cycle and answer the following questions:

1. After the reproductive or mating process, what happens to the female and male?

2. How many eggs does the female lay?

3. How big is a newborn blue-ringed octopus?

4. How big is an adult blue-ringed octopus?

5. How long does a blue-ringed octopus live?

6. What other interesting facts did you discover?

3. Have students create a slideshow or video presentation that highlights the answers to each question and any other information students learned. Ask for volunteers to share their slideshows and videos with the class.

 Do this activity in small groups of two, three, or four students.

Name: ____   Date: ___________________

Life Cycle of the Blue-Ringed Octopus

DIRECTIONS: Research the life cycle of the blue-ringed octopus and then answer the questions below. Use the answers and any other information you learn to create a slideshow or video presentation.

1. After the reproductive or mating process, what happens to the female and male?_______

   ____

   ____

2. How many eggs does the female lay? ____

   ____

   ____

3. How big is a newborn blue-ringed octopus?_______________________________________

   ____

   ____

4. How big is an adult blue-ringed octopus?____

   ____

   ____

5. How long does a blue-ringed octopus live?_______________________________________

   ____

   ____

   ____

6. What other interesting facts did you discover? ___________________________________

   ____

   ____

   ____

   ____

Writing Activities

MATERIALS

- "Vocabulary Words" worksheet
- "Describe the Picture" worksheet
- "Finish the Sentence" worksheet
- "Will I Use I-Statements When Trying to Solve a Disagreement?" worksheet
- "When I Have a Conflict" worksheet
- Pencils

TEACHER INSTRUCTIONS

1. Pass out all five worksheets for students to complete at one time, or have them complete one worksheet per day during the school week.

2. Instruct students to fill out their worksheets and be prepared to discuss their answers as a group.

3. Allow enough time for students to complete the writing activity, then review and discuss the assignment as a group.

Name: ____   Date: ___________________

Vocabulary Words

DIRECTIONS: Write original sentences that include the vocabulary words listed below. Each word needs to be used at least once, and a sentence can have more than one vocabulary word in it. When all the words have been used in sentences, draw a comic strip or a picture that represents or reflects as many of the vocabulary words as possible.

Vocabulary Words: Nice, Mean, Apologize, Problem-Solver, I-Statements, Feel, Could You Please, Stop, When, Friendship

Name: ____   Date: __________________

Describe the Picture

DIRECTIONS: Look at the picture and then fill in the worksheet.

1. This is a picture of what? ____

    ____

2. What is happening in the picture? ____

    ____

    ____

3. Where do you think this picture was taken (setting/location)? _______________

    ____

    ____

4. Write an original sentence that includes your answers to the questions above: _________

    ____

    ____

    ____

    ____

    ____

    ____

    ____

    ____

    ____

    ____

    ____

Name: ____   Date: _____________________

Finish the Sentence

DIRECTIONS: Complete the sentence and then draw a picture to match your sentence.

I WILL USE I-STATEMENTS TO ____

____

____

____

____

____

Name: ____   Date: __________________

Will I Use I-Statements When Trying to Solve a Disagreement?

DIRECTIONS: Fill in the worksheet by answering yes or no if you will use I-statements when trying to solve a disagreement. Write down three reasons to support your answer.

Name: ____   Date: _____________________

When I Have a Conflict

DIRECTIONS: Read the text and then answer the questions.

TEXT: Think about the last time you had a conflict or disagreement with a friend or classmate.

1. What was the conflict? ____
   ____

2. How did you handle or solve the conflict? _______________________________
   ____
   ____

3. Do you think using I-statements could have solved the conflict sooner and more
   peacefully? *Why?* ____
   ____
   ____

4. Why are I-statements important?____
   ____
   ____
   ____
   ____
   ____

NOTES

MANTA RAY

MURIEL, A MANTA RAY, IS VERY WISE, LOVING, KIND, AND EMPATHETIC. SHE IS A STRONG COMMUNICATOR WITH A POSITIVE ATTITUDE, AND SHE IS KNOWN AS THE PROTECTOR OF THE SEA. THE MANTA RAY TEACHES US THE IMPORTANCE OF A POSITIVE ATTITUDE AND HOW TO DEVELOP A GROWTH MINDSET.

The name Muriel means sea and bright.

Muriel Manta Ray is the greatest protector of the sea.
She is as wise, kind, and positive as one could possibly be.

Wherever she goes, she has a smile on her face.
Muriel will always stop to greet you with a warm embrace.

She always helps those in need,
and wants others to succeed.

Muriel listens to others with care,
and proves to them she will always be there.

She always acknowledges how you feel,
and shows interest in what you reveal.

She has an empathetic heart full of gold.
She is extremely strong, courageous, and bold.

Even when she is having a bad day,
she only has positive things to say.

She tells the sea creatures to find something good to focus on when they are sad.
There are countless things to enjoy and appreciate even if you're feeling mad.

It's okay to take some time to cry.
It's okay to politely ask why.

Q: You know the manta ray swims, but can it fly?

A: Yes!

You are the only creature in control of you.
And no matter what, you will always make it through.

Things can happen to cause you to feel down,
but it is your choice to smile or frown.

You're in control of your reaction,
so how will you choose to take action?

Muriel Manta Ray wonders if you'll feed your mind with negative or positive ideas.
She loves to say that tacos are delicious, but they can fall out of their tortillas.

If a mouthwatering taco can be a mess,
then a bad day here and there is nothing to stress.

A growth mindset will lead you to great success.
Think of failure as a way to show progress.

Use a few calm-down strategies to reset.
And always remember the power of yet.

Life is full of challenges, and sometimes a lot of hard work,
but having a positive attitude is a valuable perk.

Ampat Reef Diorama

MATERIALS

- Shoeboxes
- Assorted materials, such as but not limited to:
  - Markers/Crayons/Paint and Brushes
  - Construction Paper
  - Modeling Clay
  - Pipe Cleaners
  - Felt/Fabric
  - Glue/Scissors
  - Miniature Figurines of Marine Animals/People
  - Fake Plants
  - Rocks/Sand
  - Magazine Pages/Pictures

TEACHER INSTRUCTIONS

1. Have students research the Raja Ampat Reef and then create a shoebox diorama of the reef based on their research findings.

2. Instruct students to include a manta ray in their dioramas. They also can include other sea life.

3. Display the students' dioramas around the classroom and place a blank sheet of paper next to each one.

4. Have students look at each diorama and write a positive comment on the sheet of paper next to the diorama.

Muriel Manta Ray
Discussion Questions

MATERIALS

- Pencils
- "Discussion Questions" worksheet

TEACHER INSTRUCTIONS

1. Pass out the "Discussion Questions" worksheet.

2. Instruct students to fill out the worksheet by answering the questions.

3. Read the questions aloud and discuss possible answers as a group.

CLASS/GROUP DISCUSSION QUESTIONS

1. What does it mean to have a positive attitude?

2. What does it mean to have a negative attitude?

3. What is empathy?

4. How can you show others you care about them?

5. If you're having a bad day, is it okay to take time for yourself or even cry?

6. What are you in control of? Emotions? Reactions? Actions? Thoughts?

7. What is a growth mindset?

8. Is it okay to fail?

9. What calm-down strategies can you use to reset your emotions and attitude?

10. What does the "power of yet" mean?

Name: ____   Date: ___________________

Discussion Questions

DIRECTIONS: In the space provided, answer the following questions. Be prepared to discuss your answers with the group.

1. What does it mean to have a positive attitude? ___________________________
   ____
   ____

2. What does it mean to have a negative attitude? __________________________
   ____
   ____

3. What is empathy? ____
   ____
   ____
   ____

4. How can you show others you care about them? __________________________
   ____
   ____
   ____

5. If you're having a bad day, is it okay to take time for yourself or even cry?___________
   ____
   ____
   ____

6. What are you in control of? Emotions? Reactions? Actions? Thoughts? _____________
   ____
   ____
   ____

Discussion Questions continued

7. What is a growth mindset? _______________________________

____

____

____

8. Is it okay to fail? _______________________________________

____

____

____

9. What calm-down strategies can you use to reset your emotions and attitude? _________

____

____

____

10. What does the "power of yet" mean? _______________________

____

____

____

Drawing Activity

MATERIALS

- Paper/Poster Board
- "Positive Attitude vs. Negative Attitude" poster
- "Empathy" poster
- Colored Pencils/Crayons/Markers

TEACHER INSTRUCTIONS

1. Distribute the "Positive Attitude vs. Negative Attitude" and "Empathy" poster papers.

2. Review with students the directions for each poster.

3. Ask for volunteers to show and explain their drawings.

Name: ____   Date: _____________________

Positive Attitude vs. Negative Attitude Poster

DIRECTIONS: Draw a picture or comic strip of someone showing or demonstrating a positive attitude. Next to that picture, draw someone showing or demonstrating a negative attitude.

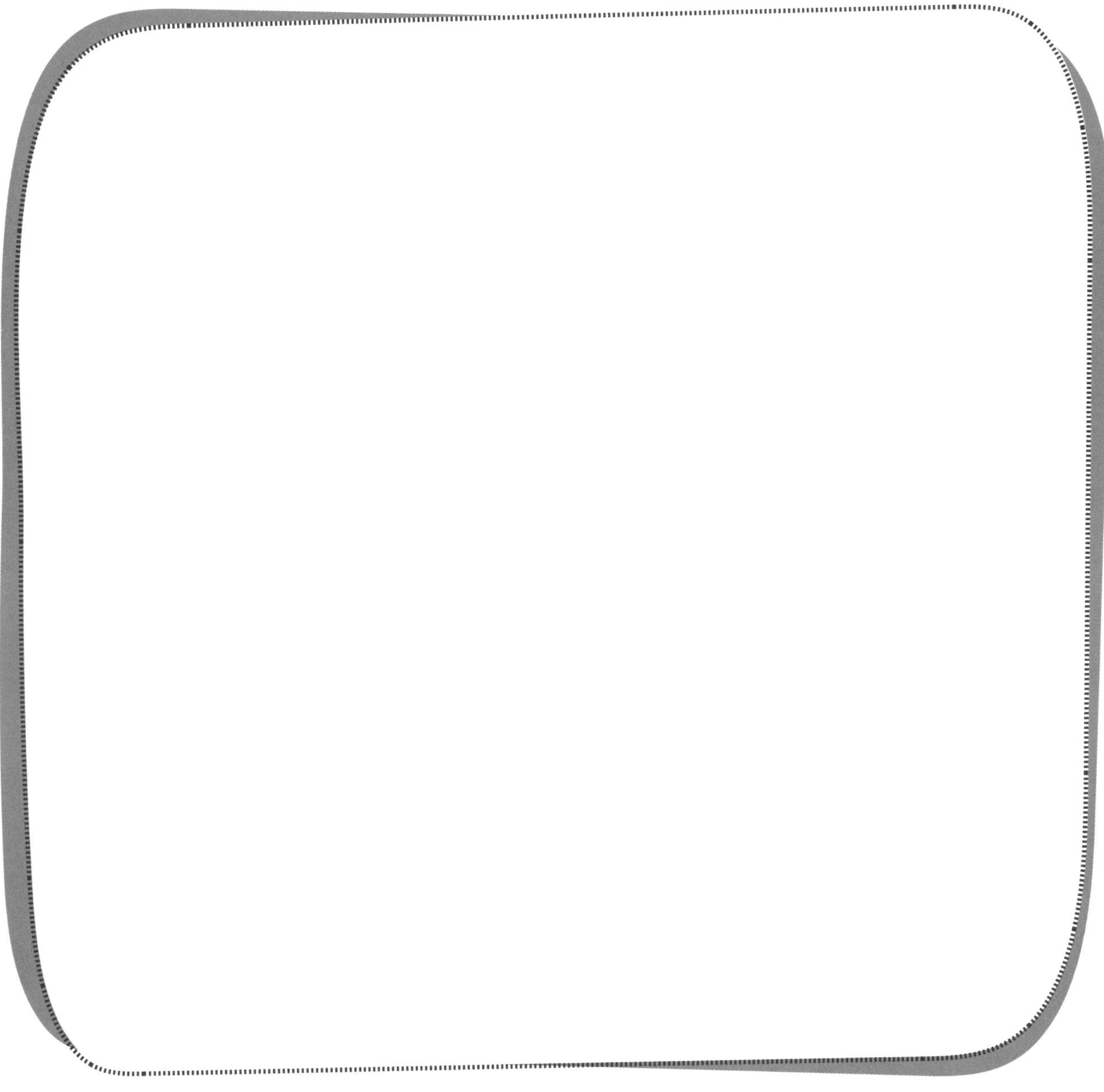

Name: ____ Date: __________________

Empathy Poster

DIRECTIONS: Draw a picture or comic strip that shows someone expressing empathy.

Manta Ray Wingspan Math

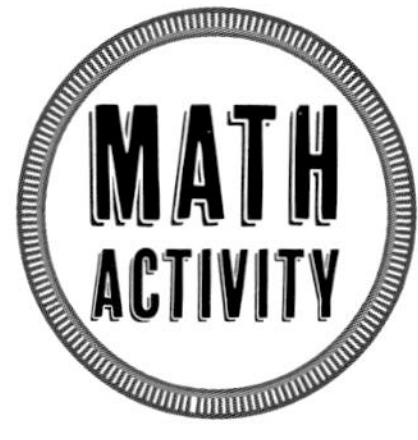

MATERIALS

- Tape measures
- Papers
- Pencils

TEACHER INSTRUCTIONS

1. Post the following math problem on the overhead or write it on a worksheet:

- The wingspan of the manta ray can reach up to 29 feet (or 348 inches). Compare the wingspan of the manta ray to your wingspan.

2. Group students into pairs, and give each pair a tape measure.

3. Instruct student A to stretch their arms out wide at shoulder height, then have student B measure student A from fingertip (left hand) to fingertip (right hand).

4. Have student B write down the length in inches, then have the two students switch positions so student A can measure student B's wingspan.

5. After all students have their wingspans measured, have them subtract their number by 348 inches to calculate the difference in wingspans.

Manta Ray Parachute

MATERIALS

- Playground Parachute (Alternative Options: Queen or King Bedsheet/Lightweight Blanket)
- Beach Balls/Lightweight Balls
- "Hidden Treasures" (Pictures/Trinkets/Seashells/Plush Toys/Objects, etc.)
- Gym/Play Area

TEACHER INSTRUCTIONS

ACTIVITY 1

1. Spread out the parachute or sheet, then ask students to lift it up and hold onto its edges.

2. Instruct everyone to raise and lower the parachute to form waves while pretending the parachute is a protective manta ray.

3. Place balls on top of the parachute, after students get the hang of making waves.

4. Tell students the balls represent other sea creatures, and their goal is to keep the balls from falling off the parachute while continuing to make waves.

ACTIVITY 2

1. Select three students to be divers.

2. Spread out the parachute or sheet, then ask the remaining students to lift it up and hold onto its edges.

3. Place the "hidden treasures" on the ground/floor below the parachute.

4. Instruct everyone holding the parachute to raise and lower it to form waves, then have the three divers run under the parachute. Each diver should grab one treasure.

5. Have the divers switch places with three students holding the parachute, then let the three new divers grab a treasure. Continue until every student has a treasure.

ACTIVITY 3

1. Assign each student the name of a sea animal (except manta ray). An equal number of students should be assigned the same name.

2. Spread out the parachute or sheet, then ask students to lift it up and hold onto its edges. Instruct everyone to raise and lower the parachute to form waves.

3. Tell students you will call out a sea animal name. When they hear their name called, they should run under the parachute and switch places with a player who has the same name. When they hear manta ray, everyone should let go of the parachute and switch sides with the players opposite them.

Freeze Dance

MATERIALS

- Music Player
- Gym/Play Area

TEACHER INSTRUCTIONS

1. Instruct students to move and/or dance around when the music begins. When the music stops, they need to freeze in position and take deep breaths until the music starts again. Students who do not freeze when the music stops, or who fall out of their freeze position before the music begins again, are out of the game and should return to their seats.

2. Ask students who are out of the game to cheer on and encourage the remaining players.

3. Change up the length of time the music plays and when it's off. This will keep students guessing.

 If appropriate, allow a student to control the music.

Science Activity

MATERIALS

- "Manta Ray Research Notes" worksheet
- Pencils

TEACHER INSTRUCTIONS

1. Distribute the "Manta Ray Research Notes" worksheet to students.

2. Instruct students to use classroom and online research tools to gather facts and information about the manta ray. Then ask them to write a short essay summarizing their research findings. Encourage students to follow the outline provided on their worksheets when writing their essays.

3. Ask for volunteers to read their essays aloud.

Name: ____ Date: _____________________

Manta Ray Research Notes

DIRECTIONS: Use classroom resources and websites to learn facts and information about the manta ray. Write down your findings in the appropriate boxes, then use that information to write a five-paragraph essay about the manta ray.

1 **Paragraph 1:** Introduction

2 **Paragraph 2:** Appearance

3 **Paragraph 3:** Habitat and Diet

4 **Paragraph 4:** Interesting Facts

5 **Paragraph 5:** Conclusion

Fun Facts about Manta Rays

MATERIALS

- "Fun Facts about Manta Rays" worksheet
- Computer/Laptop
- Internet access

TEACHER INSTRUCTIONS

1. Pass out the "Fun Facts about Manta Rays" worksheet.

2. Ask students to research fun and interesting facts about manta rays and answer the following questions:

   1. How big is the brain of a manta ray?

   2. Can a manta ray recognize itself in a mirror?

   3. How can you identify an individual manta ray?

   4. Does a newborn manta ray need care from its mother?

   5. Are manta rays dangerous to humans?

   6. What other interesting facts did you discover?

3. Have students create a slideshow or video presentation that highlights the answers to each question and any other information students learned. Ask for volunteers to share their slideshows and videos with the class.

Do this activity in small groups of two, three, or four students.

Name: ____ Date: _____________________

Fun Facts about Manta Rays

DIRECTIONS: Research facts about manta rays and then answer the questions below. Use the answers and any other information you learn to create a slideshow or video presentation.

1. How big is the brain of a manta ray? ______________________________________

   ____

   ____

2. Can a manta ray recognize itself in a mirror? ______________________________

   ____

   ____

3. How can you identify an individual manta ray? _____________________________

   ____

   ____

4. Does a newborn manta ray need care from its mother?________________________

   ____

   ____

5. Are manta rays dangerous to humans? _______________________________________

   ____

   ____

6. What other interesting facts did you discover? ____________________________

   ____

   ____

   ____

   ____

Writing Activities

MATERIALS

- "Vocabulary Words" worksheet
- "Describe the Picture" worksheet
- "Finish the Sentence" worksheet
- "Is It Important to Have a Positive Attitude?" worksheet
- "People and Their Attitudes" worksheet
- Pencils

TEACHER INSTRUCTIONS

1. Pass out all five worksheets for students to complete at one time, or have them complete one worksheet per day during the school week.

2. Instruct students to fill out their worksheets and be prepared to discuss their answers as a group.

3. Allow enough time for students to complete the writing activity, then review and discuss the assignment as a group.

Name: ____   Date: ___________________________

Vocabulary Words

DIRECTIONS: Write original sentences that include the vocabulary words listed below. Each word needs to be used at least once, and a sentence can have more than one vocabulary word in it. When all the words have been used in sentences, draw a comic strip or a picture that represents or reflects as many of the vocabulary words as possible.

Vocabulary Words: Kind, Positive, Smile, Helps, Listens, Feel, Control, Negative, Growth Mindset, Attitude

Name: ____   Date: _____________________

Describe the Picture Worksheet

DIRECTIONS: Look at the picture and then fill in the worksheet.

1. This is a picture of what? ____

____

2. What is happening in the picture? _______________________________________

____

____

3. Where do you think this picture was taken (setting/location)? ______________

____

____

4. Write an original sentence that includes your answers to the questions above: _________

____

____

____

____

____

____

____

____

____

____

____

____

Name: ____ Date: ____________________

Finish the Sentence

DIRECTIONS: Complete the sentence and then draw a picture to match your sentence.

I CAN SHOW A POSITIVE ATTITUDE BY ________________________________

____

____

____

____

____

Name: ____   Date: _____________________

Is It Important to Have a Positive Attitude?

DIRECTIONS: Fill in the worksheet by answering yes or no if you think it is important to have a positive attitude. Write down three reasons to support your answer.

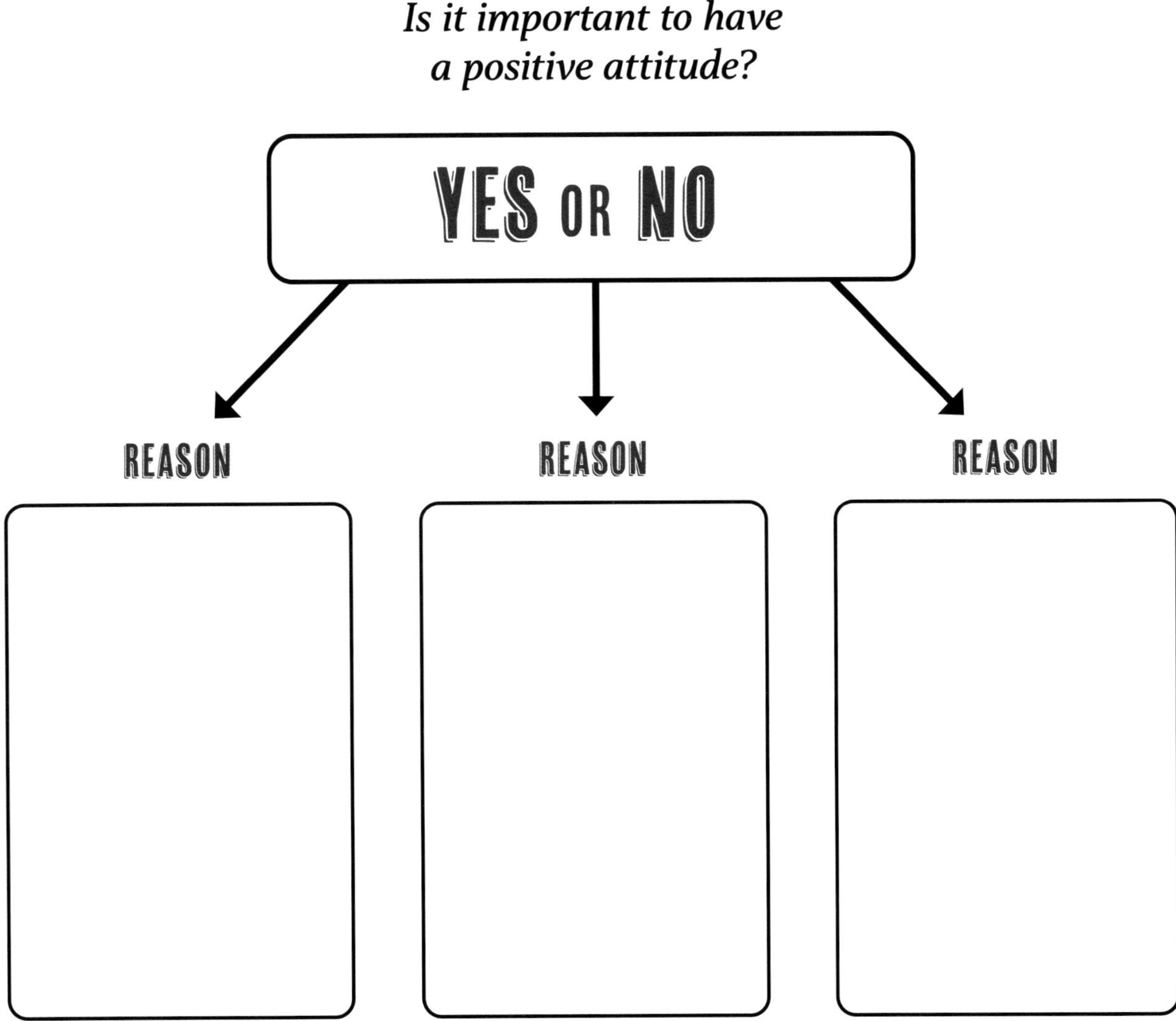

Name: ____   Date: ________________________

People and Their Attitudes Worksheet

DIRECTIONS: Read the text and then answer the questions.

TEXT: **Think about the attitudes of the people around you or people you know. Now think about someone who always seems to have a negative attitude and someone who always seems to have a positive one.**

1. Describe what it feels like to be around someone who always has a negative attitude:

    ____

    ____

    ____

2. Describe what it feels like to be around someone who always has a positive attitude:

    ____

    ____

    ____

3. Do the moods or attitudes of other people affect your mood? *If yes, how? If no, why not?*

    ____

    ____

    ____

4. Would you rather surround yourself with positive or negative people? *Explain your answer:*____

    ____

    ____

    ____

HAWKSBILL SEA TURTLE

SKILL

SHEA, A HAWKSBILL SEA TURTLE, IS HELPFUL, KIND, PROTECTIVE, AND EMPATHETIC. HE HAS A STRONG SENSE OF DIRECTION AND IS A LEADER WITH A POSITIVE ATTITUDE. HE TAKES DARIA DUGONG UNDER HIS WING, AND THEY BECOME BEST FRIENDS. THE HAWKSBILL SEA TURTLE TEACHES US HOW TO BE KIND, SHOW EMPATHY, AND MAKE NEW FRIENDS.

SEA TURTLE
Kindness

The name Shea means admirable.

Shea Sea Turtle is wise, empathetic, and kind.
He is the best friend any sea creature could find.

He is always willing to lend a hand.
He carefully listens to understand.

Shea is kind to every creature he sees.
He uses manners like thank you and please.

Shea wants to become friends with all,
no matter how big or how small.

One day, he ran into a younger creature,
who looked like she could use a wise, old teacher.

Daria Dugong was anxious, shy, and all alone.
She was the quietest sea creature Shea had ever known.

Shea took her under his wings,
and taught her all sorts of things.

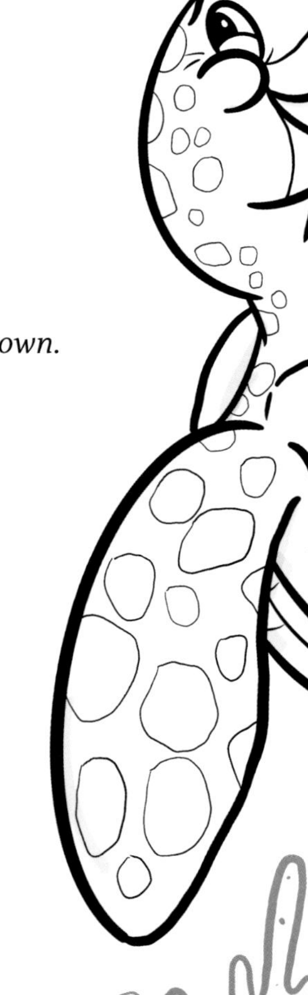

Q: What helps determine whether a
hawksbill sea turtle is born male or female?

A: Temperature

It is easy to make new friends,
using the tips that Shea recommends.

It starts with a simple smile and hello,
that will get the conversation to start to flow.

A good friend is trustworthy, honest, loyal, and caring.
They do not care what you look like or what you are wearing.

They care about what is inside,
and the kindness that you provide.

A good friend is someone who shares and takes turns.
Someone who listens to all of your concerns.

A loyal friend is supportive and will be there for you no matter what,
even if they get mad when you beat them in soccer, lacrosse, or putt putt.

A friend will cheer you on and lift you up.
When you are sad, they will fill up your cup.

Life Cycle of the Hawksbill Sea Turtle

MATERIALS

- Computer/Laptop
- Internet access
- "Life Cycle of the Hawksbill Sea Turtle" worksheet
- Colored Pencils/Crayons/Markers

TEACHER INSTRUCTIONS

1. Group students into pairs.

2. Instruct each pair to work collaboratively to research the life cycle of the hawksbill sea turtle.

3. Pass out the "Life Cycle of the Hawksbill Sea Turtle" worksheet to each group.

4. Instruct students to draw and label the sea turtle's life cycle on their worksheet.

   OPTIONAL If feasible, provide students with the necessary materials to create a three-dimensional design of the life cycle.

5. Review the life cycle of the sea turtle as a class. Ask for volunteers to show their drawings or designs to the group.

6. Ask students to provide feedback about working in pairs after they have completed the activity. Have them answer the following questions:

   1. How well did you work together?

   2. Were you kind and patient with each other? Explain.

   3. How did you support each other throughout the activity?

   4. *Add any additional questions you deem appropriate.*

Name: ____   Date: _________________

Life Cycle of the Hawksbill Sea Turtle

DIRECTIONS: Draw, label, and explain the life cycle of hawksbill sea turtles. Be prepared to show your work to the class.

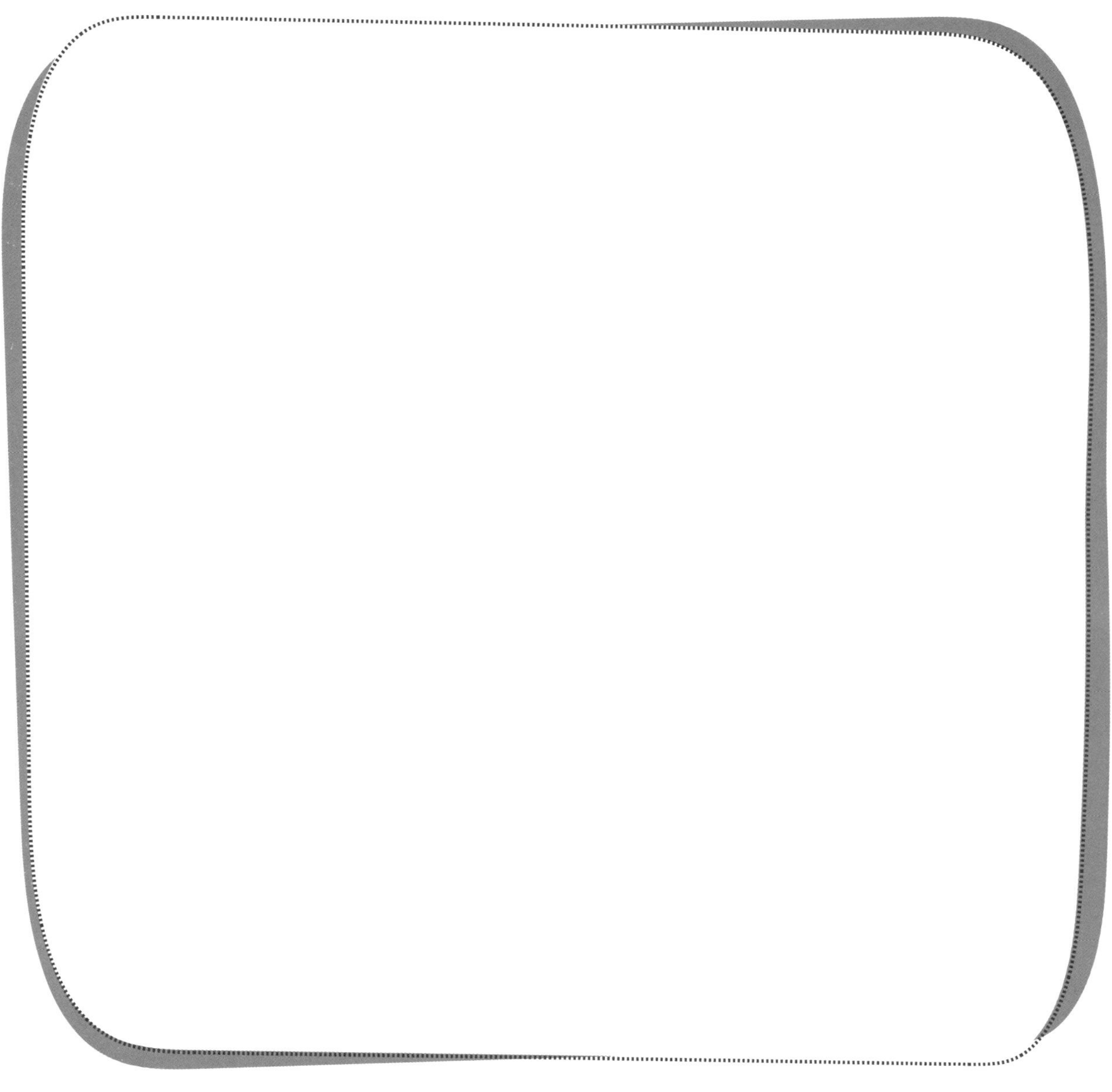

Shea Hawksbill Sea Turtle
Discussion Questions

MATERIALS

- Pencils
- "Discussion Questions" worksheet

TEACHER INSTRUCTIONS

1. Pass out the "Discussion Questions" worksheet.

2. Instruct students to fill out the worksheet by answering the questions.

3. Read the questions aloud and discuss possible answers as a group.

CLASS/GROUP DISCUSSION QUESTIONS

1. What makes someone a good friend?

2. What should you do if you see someone that looks anxious, shy, or alone?

3. How can you make new friends?

4. How can you start a conversation with someone you have never spoken to before?

5. What can you do if you want to start a conversation but don't know what to say?

6. What does it mean to be loyal?

Name: ____   Date: _______________________

Discussion Questions

DIRECTIONS: In the space provided, answer the following questions. Be prepared to discuss your answers with the group.

1. What makes someone a good friend? ____

    ____

    ____

2. What should you do if you see someone that looks anxious, shy, or alone?_______________

    ____

    ____

3. How can you make new friends? ____

    ____

    ____

4. How can you start a conversation with someone you have never spoken to before?

    ____

    ____

    ____

5. What can you do if you want to start a conversation but don't know what to say?

    ____

    ____

    ____

6. What does it mean to be loyal? ____

    ____

    ____

    ____

Drawing Activity

MATERIALS

- Drawing Paper/Poster Board
- "Friendship" poster
- Colored Pencils/Crayons/Markers

TEACHER INSTRUCTIONS

1. Distribute the "Friendship" poster board.

2. Review with students the directions for the poster.

3. Ask for volunteers to show and explain their drawings.

Name: ____   Date: __________________

Friendship Poster

DIRECTIONS: Draw a picture or comic strip that shows a strong friendship. Around the drawing or in the comic strip include words that describe a good friend, such as loyal and trustworthy.

Graphs and Charts

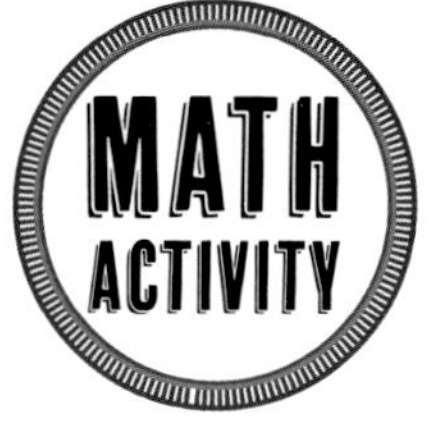

MATERIALS

- Paper
- Pencils/Crayons/Markers
- "Do You ♡ Sea Turtles?" worksheet

TEACHER INSTRUCTIONS

1. Ask students to conduct a survey to determine if their classmates, friends, and family members like sea turtles.

2. Pass out the "Do You ♡ Sea Turtles?" worksheet.

3. Instruct students to ask ten friends, classmates, and/or family members the following yes/no questions:

    1. Do you like sea turtles?

    2. Would you like to swim with sea turtles?

    3. Do you think sea turtles are cute?

4. Have students use the worksheet to collect and tally the answers to the questions. Remind them to be organized and careful when recording the responses.

5. Instruct students to make a bar graph or chart to represent the data/answers they collect, including a title for the graph and labels for the x-axis and y-axis. Then have them color the graph.

You can add or remove questions, or ask students to make line graphs, pie charts, pictographs, or other visual diagrams that best match the math concepts/skills of your class or group.

Name: ____ Date: ___________________

Do You ♡ Sea Turtles

DIRECTIONS: Ask ten friends, classmates, and/or family members the questions written below. Record their answers with a check mark or X in the appropriate box. After you have recorded all of the answers, draw a bar graph that represents the data you collected. The graph should have a descriptive title, a horizontal axis (x-axis), and a vertical axis (y-axis), each with a label describing what the axis represents.

1 Do you like sea turtles?

YES	
NO	

2 Would you like to swim with sea turtles?

YES	
NO	

3 Do you think sea turtles are cute?

YES	
NO	

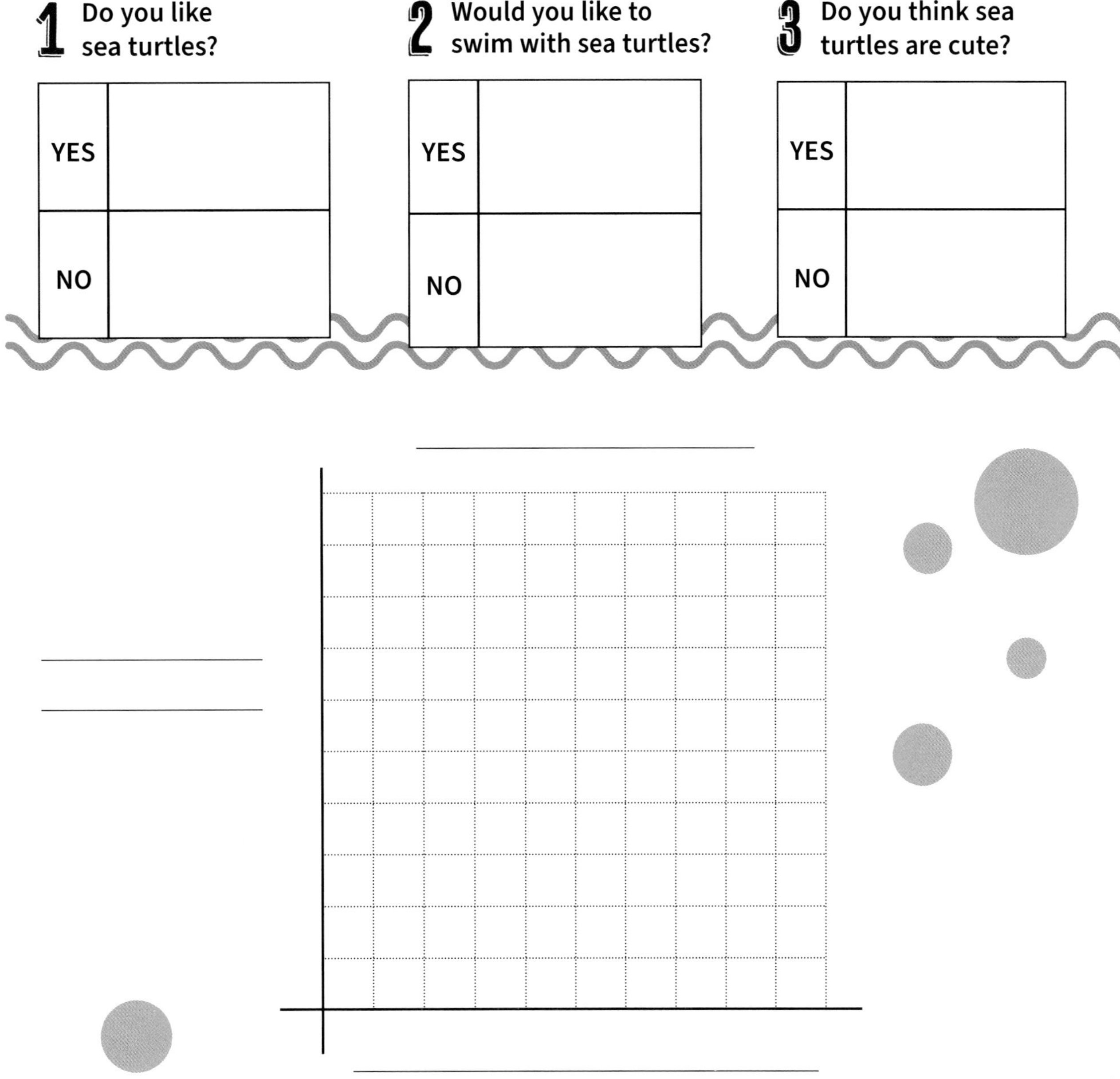

Save the Sea Turtles, Scooter Edition

MATERIALS

- Scooters
- Buckets (2)
- Plastic Bottle Caps
- Gym/Play Area

TEACHER INSTRUCTIONS

1. Divide the class into two teams.

2. Spread the bottle caps, which represent sea turtles, on the gym floor or play area.

3. Place the two buckets, which represent two oceans, on opposite ends of the gym.

4. Assign each team one of the buckets and give each team member a scooter, if possible.

5. Provide the teams with the following instructions for playing the game:

    - *"When you hear me say, 'Go,' scoot around the gym and collect as many bottle caps or 'sea turtles' as you can and place them in your team's ocean bucket. Each bottle cap represents a 'saved' sea turtle, and the team with the most bottle caps, or saves, in their bucket is the winner."*

 Modify and adjust the game based on the equipment available and the abilities of your students. Also, remind students that if they encounter sea turtles in their natural habitat, they should not touch them because it can be stressful for the animal and dangerous for the students.

Musical Dice Game

MATERIALS

- Music player
- Dice
- List of questions

TEACHER INSTRUCTIONS

1. Have students sit in a circle and then select someone to hold the dice.

2. Explain the rules of the game by saying the following:
"When the music starts, pass the dice to the person sitting next to you. Continue passing until the music stops. Whoever is holding the dice when the music stops will then roll the dice and answer a question that corresponds to the number they rolled. For example, rolling a six and a four means answering question number ten."

3. Use the following list of questions or create your own:

1. What is your favorite food?
2. How do you like to spend your free time when you're not in school?
3. What is your favorite animal?
4. If you could go anywhere in the world, where would you go?
5. What makes you happy?
6. Do you have any pets?
7. If you could only choose one, would you rather swim with sea turtles or dolphins?
8. What is your favorite sports team?
9. What do you want to be when you grow up?
10. What is your favorite movie or television show?
11. What season is your least favorite – spring, summer, fall, or winter?
12. What do you like most about school?

Science Activity

MATERIALS

- "Hawksbill Sea Turtle Research Notes" worksheet
- Pencils

TEACHER INSTRUCTIONS

1. Distribute the "Hawksbill Sea Turtle Research Notes" worksheet to students.

2. Instruct students to use classroom and online research tools to gather facts and information about the sea turtle. Then ask them to write a short essay summarizing their research findings. Encourage students to follow the outline provided on their worksheets when writing their essays.

3. Ask for volunteers to read their essays aloud.

Name: ____   Date: __________________

Hawksbill Sea Turtle Research Notes

DIRECTIONS: Use classroom resources and websites to learn facts and information about the hawksbill sea turtle. Write down your findings in the appropriate boxes, then use that information to write a five-paragraph essay about the sea turtle.

1 **Paragraph 1:** Introduction

2 **Paragraph 2:** Appearance

3 **Paragraph 3:** Habitat and Diet

4 **Paragraph 4:** Interesting Facts

5 **Paragraph 5:** Conclusion

Fun Facts about Hawksbill Sea Turtles

MATERIALS

- "Fun Facts about Hawksbill Sea Turtles" worksheet
- Computer/Laptop
- Internet access

TEACHER INSTRUCTIONS

1. Pass out the "Fun Facts about Hawksbill Sea Turtles" worksheet.

2. Ask students to research fun and interesting facts about hawksbill sea turtles and answer the following questions:

1. When did hawksbill sea turtles become endangered?
2. Why does the world need hawksbill sea turtles?
3. What are the major threats to hawksbill sea turtles?
4. What is a favorite food of hawksbill sea turtles?
5. What is the average weight of an adult hawksbill sea turtle?
6. What other interesting facts did you discover?

3. Have students create a slideshow or video presentation that highlights the answers to each question and any other information students learned. Ask for volunteers to share their slideshows and videos with the class.

 Do this activity in small groups of two, three, or four students.

Name: ____   Date: ____________________

Fun Facts about Hawksbill Sea Turtles

DIRECTIONS: Research facts about hawksbill sea turtles and then answer the questions below. Use the answers and any other information you learn to create a slideshow or video presentation.

1. When did hawksbill sea turtles become endangered? ________________________

____

____

2. Why does the world need hawksbill sea turtles? ________________________

____

____

3. What are the major threats to hawksbill sea turtles? ________________________

____

____

4. What is a favorite food of hawksbill sea turtles? ________________________

____

____

5. What is the average weight of an adult hawksbill sea turtle? ________________________

____

____

6. What other interesting facts did you discover? ________________________

____

____

____

____

Writing Activities

MATERIALS

- "Vocabulary Words" worksheet
- "Describe the Picture" worksheet
- "Finish the Sentence" worksheet
- "Would You Like to Be Friends with Shea Sea Turtle?" worksheet
- "Healthy and Unhealthy Friendships" worksheet
- Pencils

TEACHER INSTRUCTIONS

1. Pass out all five worksheets for students to complete at one time, or have them complete one worksheet per day during the school week.

2. Instruct students to fill out their worksheets and be prepared to discuss their answers as a group.

3. Allow enough time for students to complete the writing activity, then review and discuss the assignment as a group.

Name: ____   Date: ___________________

Vocabulary Words

DIRECTIONS: Write original sentences that include the vocabulary words listed below. Each word needs to be used at least once, and a sentence can have more than one vocabulary word in it. When all the words have been used in sentences, draw a comic strip or a picture that represents or reflects as many of the vocabulary words as possible.

Vocabulary Words: Kind, Friends, Always Listens, Manners, Smile, Honest, Caring, Shares, Supportive

Name: ____ Date: ___________________

Describe the Picture

DIRECTIONS: Look at the picture and then fill in the worksheet.

1. This is a picture of what? ____

   ____

2. What is happening in the picture? ____

   ____

   ____

3. Where do you think this picture was taken (setting/location)? ______________

   ____

   ____

4. Write an original sentence that includes your answers to the questions above: ________

   ____

   ____

   ____

Name: ____   Date: ____________________

Finish the Sentence

DIRECTIONS: Complete the sentence and then draw a picture to match your sentence.

I CAN BE A GOOD FRIEND BY____

____

____

____

____

____

Name: ____   Date: ____________________

Would You Like to Be Friends with Shea Sea Turtle?

DIRECTIONS: Fill in the worksheet by answering yes or no if you would like to be friends with Shea Sea Turtle. Write down three reasons to support your answer.

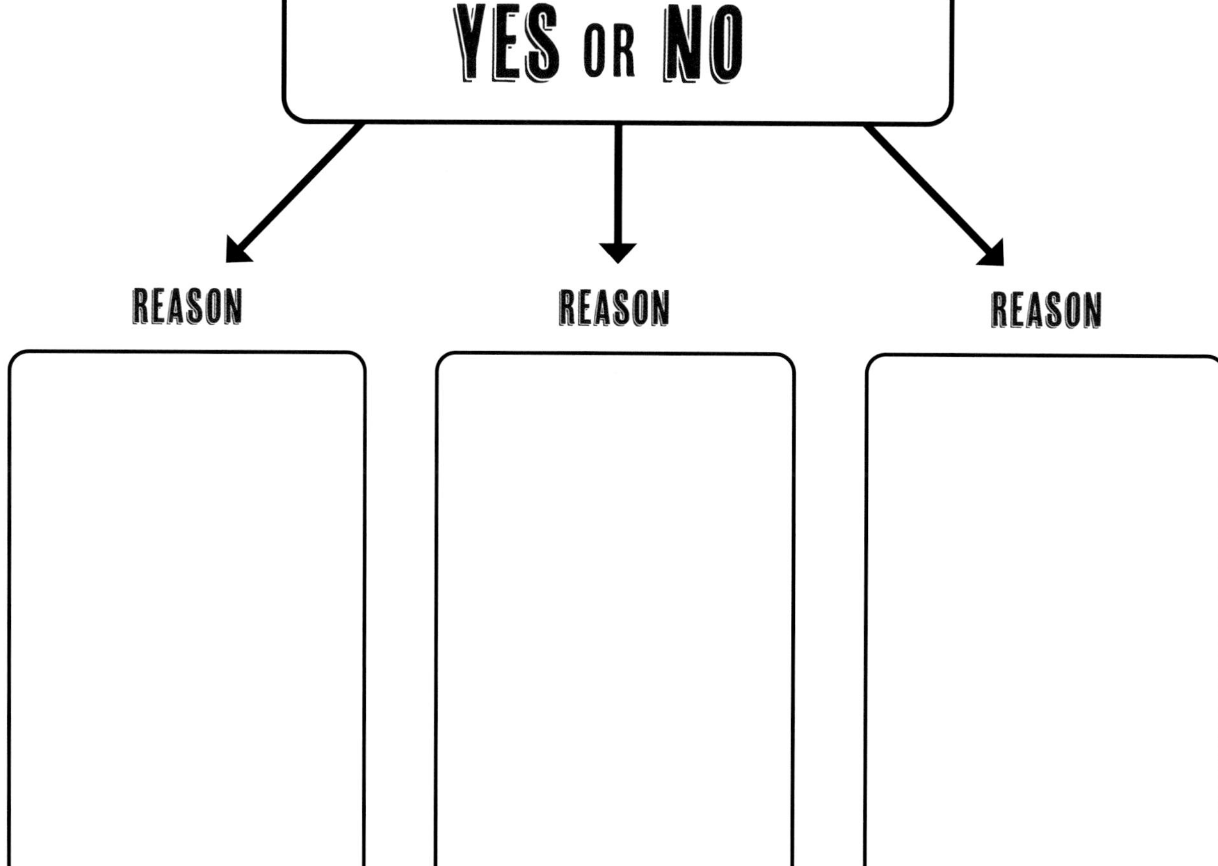

Name: ____   Date: ___________________

Healthy and Unhealthy Friendships

DIRECTIONS: Read the text and then answer the questions.

TEXT: Think about your current and past friendships. Now think about what makes friendships healthy and positive, and what makes friendships unhealthy and negative.

1. What characteristics make someone a good friend?_______________________________

    ____

2. What can lead to or cause unhealthy friendships? _______________________________

    ____

    ____

3. What can you do to be a better friend to others? _______________________________

    ____

    ____

4. What should you do if you have an unhealthy friendship?_________________________

    ____

    ____

    ____

    ____

~~~ ANSWER KEYS ~~~

DUGONG / TECHNOLOGY ACTIVITY

Fun Facts about Dugongs

Page 25

1. How can you estimate a dugong's age?
   Counting the growth layers in its tusks

2. How long can a dugong hold its breath?
   Approximately 5 to 10 minutes

3. What is the closest land relative to the dugong?
   Elephants

4. How long can a dugong live?
   Approximately 70 years

5. How much does an average dugong weigh?
   Approximately 800 pounds

REFERENCES:
https://oceana.org/marine-life/dugong/

Myers, P., R. Espinosa, C. S. Parr, T. Jones, G. S. Hammond, and T. A. Dewey. (2024). The Animal Diversity Web (online). Accessed at https://animaldiversity.org.

https://factanimal.com/dugong/

BOTTLENOSE DOLPHIN / TECHNOLOGY ACTIVITY

Sleeping Habits of Dolphins

Page 49

1. How do dolphins sleep?
   Resting at the surface, or slowly swimming near the surface

2. How long do dolphins sleep?
   About two hours at a time

3. Do dolphins close their eyes when sleeping?
   One eye remains open

4. Are dolphins unconscious or unaware when sleeping?
   No

5. Do dolphins' vision and hearing become inactive when they're sleeping?
   No

REFERENCES:
https://www.scientificamerican.com/article/how-do-whales-and-dolphin/

https://www.georgiaaquarium.org/animal/bottlenose-dolphin/

https://us.whales.org/whales-dolphins/how-do-dolphins-sleep/#:~:text=When%20sleeping%2C%20dolphins%20often%20rest,to%20the%20surface%20to%20breath.

ANSWER KEYS

BLUE-RINGED OCTOPUS / TECHNOLOGY ACTIVITY

Life Cycle of the Blue-Ringed Octopus

Page 77

1. After the reproductive or mating process, what happens to the female and male?
   Death; Females die shortly after their eggs hatch; Males die after mating

2. How many eggs does the female lay?
   50 to 100

3. How big is a newborn blue-ringed octopus?
   4 millimeters or pea size

4. How big is an adult blue-ringed octopus?
   Bodies up to 5 centimeters; Bodies and arms up to 10 centimeters, or the size of a golf ball

5. How long does a blue-ringed octopus live?
   Up to 2 years

REFERENCES:
https://www.marinebio.org/species/blue-ringed-octopuses/hapalochlaena-maculosa/

https://oceana.org/marine-life/southern-blue-ringed-octopus/

https://www.animalspot.net/blue-ringed-octopus.html#Mating_and_Reproduction

https://www.aquariumofpacific.org/onlinelearningcenter/species/greater_blue_ringed_octopus1

MANTA RAY / TECHNOLOGY ACTIVITY

Fun Facts about Manta Rays

Page 102

1. How big is the brain of a manta ray?
   Size of a fist; Largest brain-to-size ratio of any fish

2. Can a manta ray recognize itself in a mirror?
   Yes

3. How can you identify an individual manta ray?
   Spot pattern on belly is similar to fingerprint

4. Does a manta ray need care from its mother after birth?
   No

5. Are manta rays dangerous to humans?
   No

REFERENCES:
https://oceana.org/marine-life/giant-manta-ray/

https://link.springer.com/article/10.1007/s10164-016-0462-z

https://smea.uw.edu/currents/manta-rays-theyre-just-like-us/

https://www.mantatrust.org/idthemanta

https://mantaray-world.com/manta-ray-reproduction/

~~ ANSWER KEYS ~~

**HAWKSBILL SEA TURTLE /
TECHNOLOGY ACTIVITY**

Fun Facts about Hawksbill Sea Turtles

Page 125

1. When did hawksbill sea turtles become endangered?

   1970

2. Why does the world need hawksbill sea turtles?

   Help maintain coral reef health by consuming sponges

3. What are the major threats to hawksbill sea turtles?

   Hunting; Pollution; Habitat destruction

4. A favorite food of hawksbill sea turtles?

   Sea Sponges

5. What is the average weight of an adult hawksbill sea turtle?

   100 to 150 pounds

REFERENCES:
https://www.fisheries.noaa.gov/species/hawksbill-turtle
https://www.seeturtles.org/hawksbill-turtles

〜〜 TIPS 〜〜

TIPS TO SHARE WITH PARENTS

Encourage parents to support and reinforce the messages and lessons of each story at home by sharing with them these easy-to-follow tips:

DARIA DUGONG
Managing Stress and Worry

- Make sure your kids are getting enough sleep (at least 8 hours a night), and encourage other healthy habits around diet and exercise.

- Seek out "awe" moments. Whether it's a starry sky or an intricate spider web, there are many sights, sounds, and situations that can reduce anxiety and boost happiness when we make ourselves open to experiencing them.

- Help kids identify their "anchors," the people in their lives they can turn to for support and encouragement. Anchors can be a grandparent, teacher, school counselor, or any other trusted ally.

- Practice mindfulness as a family. You can practice belly breaths, read together, go for family walks, or sing silly songs.

- Reassure children that emotions are normal, and it's okay to feel not okay. Listen to them and validate their feelings. Help them to let go of the worries they have no control over and redirect them to what they can control, such as being kind toward others and having good study habits.

- Role-play handling anxious situations so kids can be more prepared to deal with them in real life. For example, if your child is anxious about giving a speech, create a mock situation with family members or stuffed animals serving as the audience. Practice different strategies your kiddo can use before the speech to stay calm, such as deep breathing, then have them practice the speech.

DUKE BOTTLENOSE DOLPHIN
Listening

- Be a positive role model. Demonstrate the listening behaviors you want (and expect) to see from your children. Maintain eye contact, ignore distractions, focus on what's being said, and use your body language to communicate you're paying attention and trying to understand.

- Play "Simon Says." This is a fun way to practice the skills of listening and following instructions while enjoying quality family time.

- Pump up the praise. When your kids practice good listening skills, praise them with words or actions. Praise can be a great way to motivate them to continue being good listeners.

- Listen without judgment. Simply listen. Remain quiet unless your child asks for input. When your child finishes speaking, express empathy or understanding and then offer guidance and support.

∼∼ TIPS ∼∼

- Encourage your kids to become active listeners by having them practice using whole-body listening (looking at the speaker, keeping their body still, remaining quiet, and focusing on what is being said).

OLLIE BLUE-RINGED OCTOPUS
Conflict Resolution and Bullying

- Role-play with your kids appropriate and helpful responses to bullying situations. Teach them how to stand up for themselves or others in positive, respectful ways. Have them practice saying "Stop" in a calm, assertive voice. Other strategies can include using humor and positive self-talk, both of which can help kids keep their emotions in check which can stop a situation from escalating even further.

- Encourage empathy and kindness.

- Help your kids use the SODAS or POP methods to strengthen their decision-making skills. When they have a problem or disagreement, have them identify or name the problem (Situation), come up with three or four possible choices (Options) for dealing with the situation, think about the pros and cons of each option (Disadvantages/Advantages), and then pick the option they think will lead to the best outcome (Solution). For younger kids, try POP. It's the same process, but shortened. POP stands for Problem, Options, and Plan. Both methods help kids clarify the problem, identify their options, and then follow through on their decision.

- Discuss the differences or nuances between bullying, a mean moment, and a conflict. Bullying is done repeatedly, and there is an unequal balance of power (social status, physical size, etc.) between the bullies and victims. A mean moment is when someone says or does something unkind on occasion, perhaps because they were having a bad day. A conflict is a disagreement or argument between two or more people, with everyone expressing their views and perspectives.

- Practice how to make feeling statements or I-statements. This can help focus your child's attention on what they feel, and helps them connect their thoughts with their emotions. I-statements should sound something like this: I feel *[emotion/feeling word]* when *[situation/problem]*. I need *[what you hope or prefer to happen going forward]*.

MURIEL MANTA RAY
Growth Mindset and Positive Attitude

- Remind kids that mess ups and mistakes are going to happen, and it can be hard to keep a positive attitude when frustrated or stressed. What's important is that they try to learn from their mistakes and reframe their thinking by remembering that most problems are temporary, and things can get better.

- Teach the power of empathy by modeling empathetic behaviors, such as giving someone your full attention and asking thoughtful questions. Teach, reinforce, and

~~~ TIPS ~~~

reward the Golden Rule, and perform random acts of kindness as a family.

- Allow failures to happen. Kids learn as much or more from their failures and setbacks as they do from their successes.

- Practice healthy calming strategies and talk about them at neutral times (when everyone's emotions are in check). Strategies can include pausing and taking three deep breaths, counting backwards, coloring, journaling, or stepping away from a situation.

SHEA HAWKSBILL SEA TURTLE
Kindness and Friendship

- Talk with your kids about what friendship means and what makes someone a good friend. Ask them how they pick their friends, and remind them that friends should make them feel big in life, not small.

- Teach the value and importance of inclusion. Always encourage your kids to be open to meeting new people, making new friends, and including others, especially those who are alone or feel left out.

- Take advantage of any opportunities where your kids can practice their greeting skills and improve their communication skills. Situations can involve anything from greeting the pediatrician at their next wellness visit to asking a librarian for assistance.

- Help your kids come up with conversation starters they can use the next time they don't know what to say to someone. Examples can include: What's your favorite school lunch? Who's your favorite superhero? Have you ever traveled outside the country?

- Praise your kids when you see them using their friendship skills!

～～ GLOSSARY ～～

Daria Dugong

Puzzled: to not understand; to be confused

Intrigued: to be curious; to be interested

Reassured: freed from worry; confidence restored

Duke Bottlenose Dolphin

Retention: to remember; to hold on to

Ollie Octopus

Strife: conflict; disagreement

Threatened: made to feel unsafe or scared; bullied

Clenched: squeezed; pressed together

Gnaw: to bite or chew

Muriel Manta Ray

Warm Embrace: a kind, friendly hug

Empathetic: to understand the feelings of others; to be kindhearted

Protector: a defender; someone who keeps others safe

Shea Hawksbill Sea Turtle

Protective: protecting someone or something; caring

Admirable: worthy of praise; having respect for someone or something